Consequences of Phenomenology

35557

Consequences
of
Phenomenology

DON IHDE

State University of New York Press

Published by
State University of New York Press, Albany

For information, address State University of New York Press, State University Plaza, Albany, N.Y., 12246

Library of Congress Cataloging in Publication Data

Ihde, Don, 1934–
    Consequences of phenomenology.

    1. Phenomenology—Addresses, essays, lectures.
I. Title.
B829.5.I32   1986   142'.7   85-9818
ISBN 0-88706-141-9
ISBN 0-88706-142-7 (pbk.)

10 9 8 7 6 5 4 3 2 1

For Dante Lenea

Contents

Preface

The central essays in this book were written for different occasions. The chapter on Ortega was for a conference at Brooklyn College on his centennial year; the chapter on Ricoeur, a symposium at the University of Toronto on his seventieth year; the chapter on Merleau-Ponty and Foucault for the Merleau-Ponty Circle; etc. When presented as a book the question is always one of what ties these separate reflections together.

The answer was provided by another kind of occasion. Richard Rorty, that *enfant terrible* of what I shall call the Analytic Establishment (which I shall hereafter dub AE), published two books during this same period, books which affected the very ways we perceive contemporary philosophy in America. The first, *Philosophy and the Mirror of Nature* (1979), revised the way in which we might understand what are commonly called Continental and analytic philosophies as the two currently dominant philosophies in America. The second, *Consequences of Pragmatism* (1982), undertook Rorty's meditations upon the state and recent history of those philosophies in the last couple of decades.

I realized that I had lived through this same history, but from a different place and a different perspective. If Rorty stood on one side of what he called the Analytic-Continental split; I stood on the other. Moreover, in his introduction to *Consequences of Pragmatism*, Rorty interprets his essays as "attempts to draw consequences from a pragmatist theory about truth." I realized that what I was doing in the essays in the center of this book was to try to draw consequences from phenomenological philosophy: hence the echo of Rorty's title, *Consequences of Phenomenology*.

Although I had heard much discussion of Rorty's two books before I had time to read them, I received something of a shock when I finally did, especially with respect to the "Analytic-Continental split" in America. For if there is a smaller, but lively "*American* Continental Establishment" (hereafter ACE), it did not occur or get portrayed in Rorty's account. *Continental* philosophers were there: Heidegger, Gadamer, Habermas, Derrida, Foucault. But not—except tucked away in

a couple of mentions—any *American* "Continentals." Thus the
history which I had experienced was *invisible*.

The split which Rorty refers to is not absolute, even if it
has been talked about for several decades. Rorty himself has
been a frequent participant in the debate, but he is not alone.
There are many others whose dominant roles have been in AE
but who have also had interest in the continental philosophies
(Peter Caws, Stanley Cavell, Arthur Danto, Newton Garver,
Charles Taylor, etc.). And the climate in which the split
occurred was first that of a crevice in an iceberg which now has
melted in some sectors, in part due to the very warmth of
controversy by the work of Rorty and others. And many of us
"Continental" Americans with analytic training have kept our
sympathies open in that direction, too.

So a reading of Rorty provided a second kind of occasion
for this collection, an occasion to similarly reflect upon the
other side of a recent history of philosophy in America, the
American "Continental" side. Its establishment, if by that one
means an organization or organizations, with a discernible
continuity and movement, effectively began when I was still a
graduate student. But the largest such organization, The
Society for Phenomenology and Existential Philosophy, decided its name in 1964, the first year I was able to attend. Thus,
enclosing the essays which independently follow consequences
of phenomenology, I decided to trace another kind of historical
reflection upon that largest minoritarian strain, American
Continental Philosophy particularly in its phenomenological
center. I conclude by returning in the last chapter to Rorty
with a suggestion about phenomenological praxis in what he
would term an edifying mode.

Readers of this book, then, will find two different types of
essays: those which are occasional and independent, united by
themes which are consequences of phenomenological investigations and, the second, an extended reflection upon the history and trajectory of phenomenology. The first are more
characteristic of works for a wider audience; the second, may
appeal more immediately to those familiar with the profession
of philosophy. This is to forewarn the reader.

With the exception of the section on Technics, the essays
for this volume appear for the first time in print. Most were
originally papers invited for particular occasions as indicated

above. Thus Chapter 1, "A Phenomenology of Voice," was an opening paper at the conference on Improvisation and Oral Tradition at the University of California, La Jolla, in 1981, Chapter 3 was part of a symposium with Hans Georg Gadamer in the Theories of Interpretation series sponsored by the Philadelphia Consortium, and so forth. However, Chapters 4, 5, and 6 have been or will be published as indicated:

"Technics: From Progress to Ambiguity" is scheduled to appear in the *Encyclopedia of Spirituality*, volume on Secular Spirituality edited by Langdon Gilkey.

"Technology: Utopia and Dystopia," was published in *Research in Philosophy and Technology*, Vol. 6, and, likewise "Technology and Cultural Variations" is scheduled for volume 8 of that series. Published here by prepermission of the editor, Paul Durbin. (Greenwich: JAI Press, 1983, 1985)

Introduction:
Phenomenology in America
(1964–1984)

It is sometimes hard to tell whether the names which are attached to philosophies occur accidentally, with malice aforethought, or carefully. Such is the problem with so-called *Continental* philosophy as designated in America. This is particularly the case when compared to the name for the dominant strains of *analytic* philosophy. First, "Continental" does not strictly compare to "analytic," since in the first there is necessarily a sense of location or origin, while in the latter the sense is more clearly that of method or, better style. Nor is this a neutral issue. For example, it has been contended that those who do Continental philosophy are necessarily trained only to deal with certain authors with the implication that Continental philosophy is a subject matter. Worse, such a subject matter precludes expertise in such areas as metaphysics, epistemology, and the like.[1] Contrarily, since analytic philosophy is a style of doing philosophy, it may range over any of the traditional subject matters. Thus, were we to apply accurate terms of comparable nature, it might be better to distinguish *Anglo*-American with *Euro*-American philosophies. Here, at least, both convey equivalent senses of origins and places. Similarly, phenomenology or phenomenological philosophy compares with analytic philosophy as different style emphases. Thus, to my mind, the by now traditional term—Continental philosophy—is a misnomer.

There is another reason why this is the case. In a world which communicates as rapidly as this and in which philosophers meet on the various continents, there is a sense in which philosophies occur everywhere, but in different mixes. For example, the Continental philosophers, Paul Ricoeur and Jacques Derrida, clearly have larger followings in North America than in their native France. Similarly, Jürgen Habermas and

1

Karl-Otto Apel are at least as well known here as in Germany. But all their philosophies belong to a markedly minority strain here. The same is the case with analytic philosophers on the European Continent. W.V.O. Quine has been discovered by some French thinkers. Ludwig Wittgenstein receives a non-British treatment in Germany, and the like. But in Europe it remains the case that this style of thinking is minoritarian and is frequently reinterpreted into the language of the tradition involved.

Nevertheless, we are faced with what are by now deeply engrained distinctions which are even classified in the American Philosophical Association's set of specializations. And what I wish to address here is a peculiar dilemma for the American versions and instances of Continental philosophy.

If one grants that what may be called the American Continental Establishment (hereafter ACE) is by now a fairly well established minority tradition in contemporary philosophy, it remains to many a kind of unrecognized presence, at least with respect to its own distinctive characteristics.

There are two reasons for this, one external, the other internal. Rorty's recent work both points to and exemplifies the external reason. What can be called the Analytic Establishment as the dominant tradition in recent philosophy, has not only opposed the inroads of Continental strains of thought, but has practiced a kind of disciplined, deliberate ignorance. Rorty in his *Consequences of Pragmatism* in an insightful chapter, "Philosophy in America Today," recognizes the Analytic-Continental split, and admits the existence of such disciplined ignorance. In characterizing AE, he indicates that many would agree with the practice of philosophers such as Reichenbach who, Rorty notes, "would approve of the widespread distrust among philosophers of those who as he put it, were trained in literature and history, who have never learned the precision methods of the mathematical sciences. He would agree with a distinguished analytic philosopher who urged that 'intellectual hygiene' requires one not to read the books of Derrida and Foucault."[2] Nor is such disciplined ignorance merely occasional. I recall in 1975 while serving on the Eastern Division APA Program Committee, several of us suggested that a seminar on hermeneutics—clearly one of the major concerns of Continental philosophy—might be of interest. A well known analytic member of that committee quickly responded, "What *is* hermeneutics?" and equally challenged, "And why is it philosophically interesting?" That a change occurred within this decade is evident from an address of a recent President of the APA in that the "hermeneuticists" were at least openly attacked and thereby recognized.[3] Today, precisely because the minority traditions in philosophy have grown in size and impact, the earlier hygiene is more difficult to maintain and is being contested within the academic-political battles which are now occurring.

Rorty himself has played a crucial role in this set of changes. His recent books are among the best introductions to the AE by one trained in the traditions of analytic philosophy. He successfully recasts the usual characterizations of Analytic and Continental philosophy into a shifted perspective which cuts across both traditions. I shall take up this analysis in the last chapter, "Response to Rorty." But while the major task of his project is addressed more to the AE than others, were one to take up either the *Mirror of Nature* or *Consequences of Pragmatism*, with all their references to the Analytic-Continental split, and thereby hope to find what goes on in American "Continental" philosophy, one would find only a passing recognition that there exists such a movement. This recognition remains on the level of "universals" in that he assiduously avoids dealing with any actual individuals in America who might practice such a style of philosophizing. Thus, functionally, Rorty continues a kind of nominalist hygiene—even if no longer a realist one—and ACE remains from his perspective *invisible*.

There is a second reason for the invisibility which Rorty gives ACE. That lies in his own philosophical selections. He is quite explicit in his lack of sympathy for or interest in *phenome-nology*. Yet, within the varieties of philosophies springing from Continental sources to America, phenomenology remains probably the strongest strain. Thus by rejecting phenomenology, Rorty ipso facto rejects much which occurs within ACE. Beyond matters of philosophical taste, this rejection is based upon his own division of philosophy into *foundational* and *edifying* types of philosophy. His argument is one which attempts to show that as a project, foundationalism is no longer tenable. Among Continental philosophers, Rorty identifies Husserl and his version of *transcendental* philosophy as foundationalist. But

then he goes on to include, at least by implication, phenomenology *in all its forms* under this category. And while not
denying that those who follow the strains of Husserl's
transcendentalism partly fit the foundationalist paradigm, this
vastly oversimplifies the situation. The "existential" and "hermeneutic" versions of phenomenology as early exemplified by
Merleau-Ponty and Heidegger, explicitly and ever more
strongly reject transcendentalism and even, in the later works,
foundationalism. It is probably the case that most American
phenomenologists are closer to these traditions than to the
earlier Husserlian one.

It is from his differentiation into foundationalism and edifying philosophy, with his emergent but perhaps reluctant
preference for the latter, that Rorty takes up his own version
of Continental philosophy. Rorty affirms that the three
greatest philosophers of the twentieth century have been
Dewey, the later Wittgenstein, and the later Heidegger. To
this group, he today adds Foucault and Derrida. All are in his
terms at least non-foundationalists. I shall take up in the last
chapter some other issues which relate to this project, but here
it is interesting to note that accidentally, if not purposefully,
Rorty's choices in effect "leapfrog" him into a very current set
of issues within ACE, but in such a way that he may miss or
ignore what happened in between.

I do not wish to be unfair to Rorty, for it was not his
purpose to either deal with Americanized "Continental"
philosophy, nor does he deal directly with phenomenology at
all as its most prominent development. But in this context, I
wish to point up factors in phenomenology with particular
emphasis upon its Americanization. This is a history which, by
fortunate historical accident, I have been able to experience.
Indeed, the two decades emphasized here have been chosen
because they span my own professional philosophical life to
date. But they also correspond closely to the life of the largest
group of Euro-American philosophers on this Continent, The
Society for Phenomenology and Existential Philosophy. (This
group actually first met in 1962 at Northwestern, but the first
widely publicized meeting, also at Northwestern, was in 1964
at which time the name was chosen. The business meeting at
that event centered around a battle over which strain of
Continental philosophy would get first mentioned. Already

then, it was apparent that phenomenology was on the rise, since the position of honor was won within its new name.)

From that beginning, with an initial membership of just over a hundred individuals, to the present, the Society has grown to be the third largest special interest group in American philosophy, with just short of 1000 persons on the mailing list. During this same two decade period, other related groups have also sprung up and taken up a kind of permanent institutional life (the list is too long to include all, but it ranges from the narrower concerns of the various "Circles"—The Husserl Circle, the Merleau-Ponty Circle—and "Conferences"— the Heidegger Conference—to other thematic groups such as the Phenomenology and Social Science group, the International Association for Literature and Philosophy, and various others.)

There has also been a diversification within ACE. Two decades ago a not unfamiliar route into "Continental" philosophy was the one which I took as an undergraduate in the late fifties. It began with existentialism. As an undergraduate what I read in philosophy classes was largely history of philosophy with large doses of Frege, G.E. Moore, Russell, and Wittgenstein. But elsewhere—sometimes in a literary context, more often through a theological connection—I had discovered Kierkegaard, Nietzsche, then Sartre, Jaspers, Buber. There was no doubt in my undergraduate mind that the questions they raised were both more crucial and more exciting than whether the morning star and the evening star had the same reference.

By the time graduate school was nearly completed, though, I had, like many others with a similar history, discovered that the insights of a Sartre and even the theology of a Tillich owed a deeper debt to another movement whose origins, at least stylistically, were closer to the "morning star" tradition. By this I mean Husserl and the origin of contemporary phenomenology. Moreover, as a student in an American graduate school, our readings were still in the history of philosophy and the dominant traditions. My official courses and seminars were more often in philosophy of language, seminars in Quine and Goodman, etc., than on Continental thinkers. What phenomenology was studied was done on the side, even underground in some respects.[4]

Original motivations often take different later directions as exemplified by the increasing move towards phenomenology from existentialism. Nor were all who came to the existential-ist-phenomenological early beginnings to come from the same direction. From the beginnings there has also been a marked affinity between the older versions of American pragmatism and phenomenology. But in the main the early devotees of Continental thought were primarily rebels against the rising dominance of AE. By the time the Society was established, many of the major graduate schools had already long been transformed into analytic centers. That movement began with the influx of a different stream of thought. For not unlike today's misnomer, "Continental Philosophy," Positivism origin-ated on European soil, notably with the Vienna Circle of the twenties. That particular brand of "Continental" philosophy, however brought with it a set of social practices and an ideology profoundly undemocratic and nonpluralistic. And even while its emigre dominated character had good external relations which defended American liberal and pluralistic politics, with respect to its internal relations within the universities, its adherents began the process of purging nonbelievers from philosophy departments, a movement which accelerated through the mid-decades of this century.[5]

Later, in spite of a neighborhood rivalry with newcomers who were Ordinary-Language heretics, by the sixties most of the "good" (elite) universities were dominated by AE. There were some exceptions even then. Yale and Northwestern became the traditional universities which favored a Conti-nental approach, and the New School for Social Research with its strong faculty of refugee philosophers also continued a non-Analytic tradition. There was also a growing influence from phenomenology in some of the Catholic universities, most obviously Duquesne and Fordham.

There had been some even earlier sporadic beginnings. Herbert Spiegelberg, reflecting upon these beginnings made a somewhat gloomy projection about the future of phenomen-ology as late as 1960:

> Phenomenology is hardly one of the leading philosophical movements in the United States, any more that it is in Britain. Judging from some recent surveys of philosophical

trends it even seems to have lost ground after 1950. In contrast to other philosophical movements recently imported from continental Europe, it has not secured a major place in the leading universities of the country. Its most outspoken representatives are to be found in Buffalo, at the New School of Social Research (formerly the University in Exile) and at some of the private Liberal Arts colleges without graduate schools.[6]

These pre-1960 beginnings I shall characterize by generations. The first members of these generations were philosophers born in the late 1890s through the early 1900s.

Interestingly, refugee scholars fleeing National Socialism in Europe constituted the largest interest group. Already here, returned from studies with Husserl, was Marvin Farber (born 1901). Not only did Farber begin to make Husserl and phenomenology known to the American scene, but he played an often crucial role in helping refugees get to this country. Unfortunately, he was also a somewhat idiosyncratic individual and thus while he was the founder of the first International Phenomenological Society, he ran the Society virtually by himself. It had but two successful meetings in the forties, and later Farber himself became more of an American Naturalist than continuing phenomenological strains.[7] Yet he was influential in helping a number of emigres to this country, most of whom were placed, as Spiegelberg observed, in four year colleges. These included Fritz and Felix Kaufman (the former did teach for a while at Buffalo) and Moritz Geiger. Spiegelberg, too, was in this wave, but taught at four year colleges until 1963 when he moved to Washington University (from whence he conducted his famous Workshops). Erwin Strauss also came to the US, and practiced his phenomenological psychology at the VAH in Lexington, Kentucky, where a series of "Pure and Applied Phenomenology" conferences drew attention. Born in this same generation, but not to arrive until later, were also two South Africans, Errol Harris and John Findlay, who were to move in the crucial sixties to Northwestern and the University of Texas, respectively. It is clear that the first generation was dominated by foreign-born philosophers.

Yet, out of this wave of newcomers only the New School was to receive a number sufficient to become anything like a center for phenomenological studies. Eventually the New School drew Alfred Schutz, Aron Gurwitsch, who joined Dorion Cairns, an American, and the continentally, but not phenomenologically oriented Hannah Arendt and Hans Jonas.[8] Others of distinction, also taught from time to time at this center which continued as a strong Continental nexus until the seventies. Unfortunately, its numbers of Ph.D.s were always small and only a few found their ways to major graduate schools. Most New School graduates, not unlike the first generation, have migrated to four year colleges.

Lewis Coser has recently published a significant study, *Refugee Scholars in America: Their Impact and Their Experiences.* In it he reinforces Spiegelberg's point concerning the relative appointments of phenomenological, as compared to positivist refugees. He argues that the reception for the positivist refugees has already been laid through the impact of British philosophy (Russell, Ayer), while and the development within pragmatism by such philosophers as W.V.O. Quine and Charles Morris as well as the logician, Alfred Tarski. In Philosophy, there was no counterpart "receiving committee".

"The logical positivists of the Vienna Circle almost all gained stellar positions in the American philosophical world, while phenomenologists and existentialists (who would come into their own only after their deaths) were reduced to academic marginality."[9] In short, the admittedly pluralistic atmosphere still discernible in the late thirties, nevertheless had a strong direction of interest towards particularly philosophy of science, logic and to a lesser degree, philosophy of language (the Philosophy of Science Association was founded in 1934, for example).

In short, the phenomenology of the earliest period simply did not "take" in an institutional way. This is not to say that the philosophers involved were not influential. As teachers, as scholars, and in some cases as original philosophers, there remains an individual impact. But born in the same era, John Wild (1902), was to later launch a second beginning. Wild underwent something like a philosophical conversion and became, in effect, an evangelist for phenomenology and existentialism. He was, moreover, located serially at three of the elite American universities: Harvard, Northwestern, and Yale. From each he spawned students who, themselves, were to be a major source of American phenomenology. There was, however, also a second generation of American philosophers, born between 1910–1920, who were to introduce the development of both phenomenology and existentialism to America. Their training was diverse, some with degrees from European universities, more from US universities. Edward Ballard, for example, settled at Tulane University and his graduates are today a strong force within ACE. He has also done his own original work in the field drawing from both phenomenological and broadly humanistic sources. William Barrett, after a career as a writer among the New York intelligentsia, became one of the most widely read introducers of existentialism in his *Irrational Man*. His NYU students constitute another group within today's ACE. William Earle played a similar role at Northwestern early, and then was joined by others with a similar set of sympathies to make Northwestern a major center in the early sixties. Quentin Lauer then with William Richardson (who later moved to Boston College) and later with Patrick Heelan formed an early set of Continentally oriented professors at Fordham. Albert Hofstadter, then at Columbia became interested in Continental philosophy, particularly the Heideggerian strain, and subsequently moved to the University of California, Santa Cruz. Also on the West Coast, Marjorie Grene played a significant role at Davis. George Schrader was already at Yale, and Nathaniel Lawrence was at Williams College. These individuals, in addition to their own philosophical work, played a most significant role in introducing the phenomenological-existential strains of thought into American philosophy by the late fifties. But in no case was there sufficient grouping to create anything like a major center for Continental philosophy at this time.

In spite of this lack of critical mass, the next generation of ACE philosophers was again larger in number, the generation born between 1921–1930, most of whom gained degrees in the fifties. Their alma maters were diverse, but two identifiable sources begin to show themselves. First, Americans began, in this era, to migrate to the Louvain where the Husserl Archives had been established and where there existed a group of second generation European scholars who continued the European traditions in phenomenology. Graduates of the

Louvain from this time, into the next generation, rose to prominence in ACE. These include the names of James Edie, one of the major founders of SPEP and also of crucial importance in bringing Northwestern into existential-phenomenological visibility in the sixties, later, also from the Louvain, Patrick Heelan, and then, born in the next generation, Alfonso Lingis and Robert Sokolowski.

Others, already in this generation, show early connections to John Wild, notably Frederick Olafson, Calvin Schrag, Samuel Todes, and Hubert Dreyfus; to some New School connections, although with a degree from Nebraska, Maurice Natanson; others with European degrees, Joseph Kockelmans, Rome, and J.N. Mohanty, Göttingen. John Compton, Yale, and Eugene Kaelin, Illinois, were also of this generation.

This brings us to the generation of philosophers born in the thirties (1931–1940). The list of productive, "Continentally" oriented philosophers in this group is potentially too large to do more than sketch the major outlines of the generation. First, with a few exceptions previously noted (Lingis and Sokolowski), most of the inhabitants are American educated. Second, connections to the earlier generations are more clearly marked. Third, this now largest generation, dominantly American educated, began to extend phenomenology both into new areas and with certain distinctive characteristics born of the work of the earlier generations.[10]

The names I mention here are at best suggestive. The list is not intended to be comprehensive nor am I yet differentiating between those who would stand out as research program oriented as contrasted to scholars. But in each case the names would be easily recognized within ACE circles. One set of names are Barrett students, notably Bruce Wilshire, Charles Sherover and Jose Huertas-Jourda. Northwestern students appear in this decade, including Edward Casey and Paul Brockelman. Yale, by this time, has also emerged as a major producer of ACE scholar-philosophers, many of whom are today placed in major graduate centers, including David Carr, Charles Scott, Karsten Harries and Erazim Kohak. The New School produced Richard Zaner in this period, and Lester Embree, both now in graduate programs. Edward Ballard's students constellate another grouping with John Sallis and Harold Alderman from this period, both with substantial publication records, and later Bernard Dauenhauer. Other names are from scattered sources, including Arnold Berleant (Buffalo), David Levin and Joan Stambaugh (Columbia), John Caputo (Bryn Mawr), Peter Koestenbaum and myself (Boston). Duquesne, in its first phase, also produced a number of students, including Theodore Kiesel, Garth Gillan and David Krell. While there are many more individuals who might be named here, it is to be noted that this is the generation of degree candidates from the sixties, the first "boom" generation of ACE philosophers.

This brief detour into the pre-1964 background of Continental philosophy, now brings us back to the institutionalized beginnings of ACE. Fortunately, not all trends within the universities were with the traditions which sought to narrow the idea and practice of professional philosophy to a single lineage. Students, many individuals in other disciplines, and a wider readership all helped reinforce for publishers that books in phenomenology and existential philosophy sold well. Northwestern as an early focal point capitalized upon this fact and the series in phenomenology and existential philosophy became one of the most successful philosophy series in America. Later a number of other university presses also established Continental series and commercial houses also joined in with publications by at least leading individuals (for example, Harper and Row and the Heidegger books). Today the majority of major university presses include such titles in their lists or have their own Continental series. I refer to this phenomenon to indicate that while some within the profession would have preferred invisibility for Continental philosophy, a certain spreading interest occurred anyway, perhaps in part because of the self-consciousness which arises among minority groups.

At the same time, I indicated above, there have been both external and *internal* reasons which have mitigated against the recognition of a distinctive American version of "Continental" philosophy. Part of the reason for this lies with some of the working habits—or as I shall call them, *secondary style characteristics*—of the philosophers who work in this tradition. Philosophical styles may be noted to follow what Kuhn would call *paradigms*. But in this case a paradigm is not often explicit; it is, rather, implicit in a set of practices which operate at different levels. Indeed, what is taken as an explicit ideal, often varies considerably from the implicit practice which results.

Rorty, again, provides us with such an insight with respect to what has happened in AE. The positivist forebears of AE admired what could be called a "science paradigm." Its watchwords were "rigor," "precision," a thinking modelled upon mathematics and strict logics, and a model which could be called a *research program*. But a question can arise as to whether or not another aspect of the science paradigm holds: is the research accumulative? That the practices have been sharpened, even extended to realms of interest previously barred by the secret metaphysical tastes of the Positivists, can hardly be denied. But one would be hard put to draw up a set of agreed upon results with respect to the research program paradigm. There is something short of a "normal science" product within AE. Indeed, such a lack is one of the reasons Rorty himself takes to justify shifting to a more modest notion of philosophy as edifying. If the explicit paradigm is that of a scientifically idealized research program, what became of the practice was something different. What emerged in practice is something much more like a legal paradigm, as Rorty citing Moulton, points out. Moulton calls this the *Adversary Method*: "Within the Adversary Paradigm we understand earlier philosophers as if they were addressing adversaries instead of trying to build a foundation for scientific reasoning and to explain human nature. Philosophers who cannot be recast into an adversarial mold are likely to be ignored."[11] As a description of late twentieth century Analysis, this paradigm makes much more sense than the earlier explicit "scientific" one. It also accounts for the current willingness of the analytic philosopher to pronounce upon (as a "legal opinion") virtually any and all subject matter. His or her task is simply to translate that subject matter into analytic "legalese."

Similarly, in a general sense, philosophers who practice in the Continental mode, also have a traditional paradigm. That paradigm taken most generally is more "literary" if by that one means *textual* and *historical* criticism. In this sense, Reichenbach was right, that such philosophers were trained in literary and historical modes (pluralistically, of course, one question is simply: why not have several paradigms operating at the same time?) More to the point, however, such a paradigm might be better characterized as a *scholarship* rather than a (scientific) research model. This is to say that the tools are necessarily the languages (French, German, whatever), the in-depth knowledge of the history of (idealism, transcendentalism, whatever), and of the internal intricacies of the texts involved. Given such a scholarly paradigm and the intellectual's penchant for flouting the tools of the trade, it is no wonder that one finds some Continentally oriented philosophers playing with foreign words, citing by memory "paragraph X of S's work," and drawing connections and criticism by historical, exegetical deftness. Furthermore, one could predict, from these contrasting paradigms, what some of the battle characteristics would be between the two traditions. From ACE to AE, accusations would include: He/she doesn't even know German." "He/she has not even read Hegel." "How can he/she say that, when it's apparent that the text has never been understood?" Contrarily, AE to ACE: "There's not an argument in all that he/she has said." "Have you asserted anything at all?" "Can that be made clear, or is it just some obscure and impossible idea?" We have heard this all before and at this level it remains a non-conversation since each is simply re-asserting his or her paradigm ideals.

This generalized practice in some degree characterizes virtually all the philosophers who practice philosophy in an ACE mode (as well as their European counterparts). But while expertise in such a practice is a necessary condition particularly for *scholarly* philosophy, it is not necessarily a sufficient condition for "philosophy" as it has become thought of in the twentieth century. Nor is this all that occurs within ACE. For in spite of the conflicting habits which tend to obscure results, I shall contend that something which is distinctive to "American" continental philosophy has occurred.

In the American professional and dominantly analytic context, however, the generalized Continental paradigm poses a serious problem. The problem is not merely one of interstylistic communication. It is one which is an emergent from the critical-historical paradigm itself. Implicit in the historical-critical practice, is a focus upon what has been done, most concretely and in most instances, upon what/who said. Thus for the most part, the scholarly paradigm is one which in practice focuses upon philosophical giants. Giants, however, are rare and occur not even with every decade. But at least they are well recognized. Thus American Continental philosophers will be found primarily dealing with those giants. In phenomenology the current classical giants are of course Husserl, Heidegger, Merleau-Ponty (with others coming and going in favor, for example, Sartre, Scheler, etc.). And virtually every ACE philosopher will cite, interpret, criticize the giants. Then what happens is that once a set of giants appears, there follows a generation or two of interpreters. Or, contrarily, if there are living giants, a community of respondents.

At the same time this practice produces a secondary result. It may be symptomatically located in citation practices.[12] For example, let us say that in a given year some twenty philosopher-scholars write something on one or more giants— what is interesting is that few of these scholars will cite each other (there are exceptions, but I am talking about dominant tendencies). Thus I can pick up virtually any journal in this tradition and find that the footnotes are all pointing *back* to the giants, with very little horizontal reference. But this means that those who are contemporary are, functionally, *invisible* to each other. So, in print, it is almost as if nothing has happened since the giant's work. The point here is not at all to urge that commentator scholars start citing each other with regularity— were that to be the case we would simply have a Talmudic, additive tradition which would be at the least, cluttered!

The citation pattern in AE, however, is radically different and inverse from the same practices in ACE. Rorty's two books are perfect examples of that practice. Most of his citations are *horizontal*. Not only is virtually every currently working analytic philosopher of importance cited, and those with almost as much frequency as the giants (in *Mirror of Nature*, for example, Donald Davidson approaches Dewey in numbers of references) but we get the sense that the debate or research program is strictly contemporary. Even his giants, Dewey, Heidegger, Wittgenstein, are given an aura of pastness. In contrast, in ACE one finds a sense that the giants are perhaps the only ones living, almost always referred to as present! Moreover, these references are done usually with deference such that the references are both references *to* giants, and recognition *as* giants.[13]

Then in AE practices, not only is there a tendency to deal

with strictly current research programs (have readers detected that now even Wittgenstein belongs to a "classical" period, *as past?*), but the adversarial practice as in law, tends to make any arguer "equal" to the adversary, no matter how absurd this might seem. These comparative differences are deeply established working habits. And they are habits which, between styles, disadvantage the clear emergence of a research program approach recognized within the ACE.

I am not here trying to play down the importance of philosophical scholarship. On that level ACE has played an important, even essential role. Translation and introductory exposition have always been basic. This task characterized much of the early work of the Northwestern series and today continues with the diversification of the Continental traditions into their "post-phenomenological" phases. Moreover, larger historical, interpretative works have also been significant contributions to understanding whole movements, as Richard Palmer's *Hermeneutics* or the even larger *The Phenomenological Movement* by Herbert Spiegelberg. But what I am after is what might be called the original and distinctive within the American phase of Continental philosophy, particularly as it begins to approximate a research program paradigm.

By selecting this narrow focus, a focus which grants a certain privilege precisely to some AE aims, I have created a more difficult task. The task is difficult not only because it cuts across the dominant grain of ACE practice, but because of the historical reasons cited above. Both in mass and chronology, ACE philosophers remain smaller in number and have had a shorter time to attain some kinds of visibility. It is debatable, for example, that there are any *world-class* American "Continental" philosophers. Not that there are lacking either internationally known or renowned philosophers in ACE. Nor, when one compares generationally, it is obvious that there are many—*if any*—world-class AE philosophers, particularly when one calls for world-class to be influence beyond English language circles. AE philosophers who might be world-class might well include Quine, Davidson, Chisholm and Sellers— but if this is the case, one must note that they belong to the generation of the teens. They thus precede by a decade or more the first graduates of any ACE graduate centers which could have produced similar philosophers. In fact, it was only in the sixties, that there emerged sufficient depth in America for proper training of philosophers in the Continental traditions in America—fully two decades after the most notable AE philosophers mentioned above received their degrees.

Not only has the movement been hampered by a lack of graduate schools which emphasize Continental philosophy, but if the first decades of the institutionalized form of professional philosophy was necessarily dedicated to importation tasks such as translation, interpretation and dissemination, then only by the mid-seventies could one begin to realistically expect results. Within such bodies as the American Philosophical Association's Nominating Committee, it is widely held that philosophical maturity is only attained by one's mid-fifties.[14] This, if true, means that the larger numbers of ACE philosophers have yet to arrive. AE, in contrast, is more than a decade older and has been producing graduates for that length of time. Not surprisingly, if there are some world-class AE philosophers, one would not necessarily expect the same to be the case with ACE until this era. The sixties then, became crucial in this history in part because during that decade the first traditional graduate schools began to produce American trained ACE philosophers. Yale and Northwestern rose to Continental prominence during that decade and it was something of an inside joke to speak of the "Yale-Northwestern Axis" to describe the power centers which also dominated SPEP. Northwestern was first dominant, and drew the constellation of James Edie, Earle Harris, John Wild to join William Earle already there. Later, when Wild moved to Yale, another grouping gelled, although somewhat more discontinuously, with John Findlay later, and the younger scholars Karsten Harries, Edward Casey and David Carr, aided by veterans like George Schrader. Simultaneously, alongside more traditional Thomist and historical interests, several Catholic universities developed strong Continental emphasis, most notably Fordham and Duquesne. One of the two, Duquesne became the most Continentally concentrated with both philosophy and psychology, but in two phases. The earlier phase saw a series of Dutch scholars come and go of whom Andre Schuwer remains, but which then also included Alfonso Lingis.

By the late sixties, through moves within academic and the beginning influx of sixties degree candidates, other schools also began to rise to prominence as having Continental constellations. It is to be noted, however, that in almost every case this was done in the context of a broadly pluralistic department, often one which emphasized the history of philosophy which was also something of a dying specie in that era. Thus Lingis and Kockelmans moved from Duquesne and Pittsburgh, respectively, to Pennsylvania State University, to join John Anderson and then Thomas Seebohm (a more recent German arrival) to begin a shift of "Continentalism" to mid-Pennsylvania. Vanderbilt also soon rivaled Tulane in the South, eventually including John Compton, Charles Scott, and a number of Yale graduates including other Wild students like Robert Ehman. At the end of the sixties, while Yale and Northwestern retained dominance, there were now enough other places where more than single individuals could begin to produce graduate students who would just now be expected to begin to surface.

Given the normal time required for one to attain tenure and become a recognized scholar, it was to be expected that the large class of the sixties would just recently have come to the philosophical maturity needed to make a major impact. Given the larger numbers already noted, and their placement in every region of the US and Canada, precisely that began to happen.

Politically, this growing momentum was evidently felt by AE, because the decade of the seventies begins to mark the time of a certain contestation and the emergence of what Rorty calls the Analytic-Continental split. Several symptomatic events happened simultaneously. First, Yale and Northwestern came under fire both from without and within by individuals concerned to have a stronger visibility for analytic philosophy in these schools. The result, over the decade, was that both began to lose some of the strength in Continental philosophy which had been previously taken for granted. Second, the austerity era of higher education budget cuts along with the "overproduction" of Ph.D.s drew the interests of legislatures and boards of regents anxious to cut back costs in doctoral programs. This was the very period in which Stony Brook decided to develop a new doctoral program, deliberately designed to include a strong Continental component.

It was also a period of strong contestation, first from AE voices associated with the American Philosophical Association,

later within the highly controversial State Education Department reviews of New York State which resulted in the demise
of the New School as a doctoral program and in whose wake
the so-called pluralist movement arose. In spite of this, 1971
saw the beginnings of a program which was by this date to
constellate a group of eight American Continental philosophers within the Stony Brook program. Interestingly with
respect to Rorty's configuration of twentieth century giants,
the structured pluralism of Stony Brook divided its "wings"
into analytic, Continental and historical-systematic groups, the
latter of which was largely out of pragmatist roots. In any case,
by 1983, James Edie in his address on the state of Continental
philosophy in America, acknowledged that the primary centers
of ACE had shifted to Penn State and Stony Brook.[15] These
centers, however, did not replace the others mentioned which
remain multifaculty sources for graduate education.

If the sixties were the first "boom era" for American
phenomenology, the seventies marked a shift of where the
centers could be found, but also of a proliferation of
Continental philosophies in America and the subsequent
development of multiple strands. Today virtually no self-
respecting graduate school in philosophy totally lacks representation in Continental philosophy. In some cases that representation is minimal; in others carefully taught by persons
having the correct AE credentials; but in others by individuals
who, like Rorty—to whose name we might add with equal
notable claim, those of Charles Taylor and Stanley Cavell—
came to interests in Continental philosophy out of their own
philosophical development from within AE itself.[16] The
disciplined ignorance of the past must now appear simply as
ignorance. In part this development is due to the often less
noted, but growing labor of ACE philosophers, sometimes
directly, at other times indirectly. One such mode of indirect-
ness has been not dissimilar to my own previous experience.
The army of teachers who have sometimes taught simply the
text of giants, did stir the imaginations of more than two
decades of students who have taken it upon themselves to
demand more. Similarly, through interdisciplinary impact,
phenomenology in particular, has created a broader spectrum
of interest. This, such that hygiene could no longer be
effective.

The story does not end there, however. The seventies were busy in other respects as well. In Europe, it can safely be said that the era of "classical" phenomenology has eclipsed particularly if by that is meant the foundationalism of a Husserl or even the early debates from both Heidegger and Merleau-Ponty against the last vestiges of early Modern philosophy (itself foundationalist). I shall return to this theme in my response to Rorty for there is a sense in which he comes to this debate *too late*, but here I wish to make a more historical point concerning Continental philosophy in its relation to the American continent. The "post-phenomenological" period in Europe is marked by a proliferation of related philosophies which also began to make serious impact in the seventies. Of these the hermeneutic traditions and the traditions which run in French philosophy from the structuralists through decon-struction, to which must be added the neo-Marxian combina-tion of phenomenology and political thought known as Critical Theory, are the most important. All of these movements began to be imported strongly in the seventies.

Each of these new movements, while related to and often dependent upon "classical" phenomenology, are in their own way critical of phenomenology. But the basis of the criticism is essentially different from that which arises from analytic philosophy. Given what I have said above about the secondary style characteristics of ACE philosophers, one might expect that the ways in which these new strains are received will initially follow certain patterns. That this is the case may be indicated by some of what happened in the seventies regarding the new wave of European thought.

First, there emerged a new set of European giants; the "later" Heidegger, Hans Georg Gadamer, Paul Ricoeur, all associated with hermeneutics. Then, Michel Foucault and Jacques Derrida as the most notable in the French structuralist-deconstructionist style. And Jürgen Habermas and Karl Otto Apel as the most obvious pair in the Critical Theory traditions. Second, we can expect there to be a younger generation of scholars who will do the initial work of introducing inter-preting, translating, and even evangelizing for this new gener-ation of giants—and that is certainly the case. From this group, however, one can expect new research programs and original thought to emerge as well. But its most distinctive character may not yet be visible enough to discern at this early stage. It is, however, important to note the emergence of a now multi-layered tradition.

I am not here suggesting that we will now have to expect another decade before such programs emerge. For while there is an initial chronological sense in which any new intellectual revolution must go before it is easily extended, much which is original begins to occur *through* the scholarly paradigms which still dominate ACE philosophy. That stage is the way in which the new thoughts will be digested—although some will not produce a full result, others will follow through.

This development brings us to the present, the eighties. This decade has seen the acceleration of interest in the wider variety of Continental philosophies and has been marked by several tendencies. First, there has been the strong impact of the hermeneutic/deconstructionist debate. Associated with this debate has been the spread of its focus—texts, narratives, the role of artist vis-a-vis critic, etc.—to the literary world. Paralleling this impact, however, has also been an important set of events which have been directed to the younger generations of analytic philosophers, retraining them via the summer seminar. Here Rorty, Dreyfus and John Compton have played crucial roles. The eighties are seeing a diversification of Euro-American philosophy.

Are these developments still imports? And are the philosophers who first do the reading and interpreting limited to *scholarly* tasks only? It is here that a few remarks about the presumed scholarly paradigm may be appropriate. Because my own training has been more traditionally analytic than not, and my paradigm sympathies, if there be such a thing, tend toward the research program model, my colleagues frequently remind me that I am unfair to the scholars and lack the perceptions to note what is original inside this practice.

Scholarship has its own justification. Translation, introduction, interpretation (which can be creative too) are necessary tasks and they are, particularly for ACE traditions, necessary as tools. All of us operate at some time or other in this mode. Nor is this all that happens within the best instances of the scholarly paradigm itself. Philosophical issues, *philosophy* is also done *through* this more historical mode. Creative rereadings, reconstructions, and new histories emerge. This is the center of the generalized Continental paradigm at its best and characterizes much of what even the giants do. But in this case the imitators of giants frequently fail and become merely technical manipulators of others' ideas—that is too often the case with ACE philosopher-scholars. And, finally, there is a third sense in which through rereading and critique, by contrast a new program can emerge, either as an extension into a new area, or by means of selective rejection and new insight, go in another direction. This is critique for the sake of movement, and again exemplifies one of the better possibilities within ACE tradition. None of the above are in the narrowest sense what I have in mind as a research program paradigm, although such a model may often relate to the above practices. Beyond all of these moves, I would hold that a research program paradigm is one which explores new areas, creates new perspectives, makes something like a gestalt-shift possible, and the like. In short, it is what happens through the work of philosophers like Heidegger who transforms whole domains of the way in which we experience things; or Kuhn and Foucault, who so radically redo their subject domains that one may detect a disjunction in the very history of interpretation of those domains. Has such work occurred with ACE? I contend, without necessarily implying the same magnitude, that such results have already occurred and are now occurring within the precincts of ACE.

What I wish to point to are distinctive programs and areas of philosophical development, which while within the traditions and style of Continental, particularly phenomenological philosophy, are original contributions on their own and not mere repetitions or extrapolations of the thought of others. There is some academic risk in such an assessment precisely because it is essentially evaluative, selective and related to the evaluator's perceptions. Thus the examples I cite—while I think they would be widely acceeded to by peers—are in no way exhaustive, although they may be considered representative.

If guided by citation indices of recent years, one cannot but take note of the prominence of Maurice Natanson, who while clearly prodigious in publication, scholarly beyond doubt, willing to footnote, interpret and criticize the giants, has nevertheless attained his own stance and impact. Although he was the only ACE philosopher to win a National Book Award (for his work on Husserl) which would mark him as a scholar-philosopher, to my mind his own work shows through his development of the concept of social role. Beyond Schutz and Sartre, his acknowledged mentors, Natanson has had dramatic impact not only within philosophy, but like many phenomeno-logically oriented thinkers, upon the human sciences.

Of a different stripe entirely one must also take note of Hubert Dreyfus whose communicative role has been both an openness to AE and with an argumentative style which parallels AE type philosophy. Probably more than any single individual (although Charles Taylor and Richard Rorty have played similar roles), Dreyfus has radically translated Continental philosophy into an idiom understandable by AE thinkers. His impact upon philosophy of language via his colleague, John Searle, is but one example of this effect. But most originally and even notoriously, Dreyfus's work on computer "cognition" and artificial intelligence has given him a unique place among ACE philosophers. This is work beyond the ken of a Husserl or a Merleau-Ponty and is, perhaps, one mark of a certain American willingness to explore unorthodox (for philosophers) areas.

Two philosophers in a more traditional mold, almost classical in form but of highly recognized profiles are J.N. Mohanty and John Sallis.

Mohanty is an examplar for dealing with philosophical issues through critique and extension. His issues are those which fall directly between phenomenology and analysis, such as problems of reference and intentionality reflected via Husserl and Frege, and his prominence is a growing one respected within the more open-minded domains of AE. John Sallis is a counterpart with respect to extention through reinterpretation and reformulation, particularly with respect to the history of philosophy.

Robert Sokolowski, clearly one of the most original and autonomous of the American phenomenologists, although starting from a Husserlian base, has taken his own research programs into philosophy of language, ontology and ethics. His *Presence and Absence* and *Husserlian Meditations* are already regular readings in many seminars.

Now maturing, the work in philosophy of perception

published by my colleague, Patrick Heelan, in his *Space Perception and the Philosophy of Science*, clearly refines, extends and goes beyond much of the earlier work of Merleau-Ponty. He has been able to relate this essential phenomenological approach both to the formalism and the mathematization of the sciences.

In the six cases just mentioned, I would contend that all are noteworthy by the usual scholarly community standards (cited, invited, reviewed, and criticized). Each, while having different focal concerns and background figures, has gone on to develop a unique and original position not reducible to the work of the background giants. The same applies to others not mentioned here, but who like the small sample noted, undertake research programs with original impact. But what I am after is the isolation of a pattern of research distinctive of the *Americanized* version of phenomenology.

There is a sense in which phenomenology may be said to have a "body/body" problem rather than a "body/mind" problem. From Husserl's lived body through Merleau-Ponty's *corps vecue*, even in Heidegger's highly spacialized Dasein, the problem is always one of an experiential, concrete embodiment. Richard Zaner has taken this clue and developed a trend in philosophy of medicine, which rather than emphasizing the popular applied utilitarian ethics to medical problems, has related the phenomenological self-body to medical models.

Bruce Wilshire, himself an actor, as well as philosopher, has taken the notion of phenomenological variations into a study of the theatre and theatrical role in his *Role Playing and Identity*. Bernard Dauenhauer has taken the difficult problem of silence and related it to ontology. Edward Casey has produced a masterful work on the imagination which reviewers have claimed has exceeded Sartre's earlier work. David Carr has taken Husserl's concept of both temporality and the lifeworld into the problems of the philosophy of history in a unique way. Calvin Schrag, whose work has been on the foundations of the social sciences, has also been particularly visible through his series of National Endowment for the Humanities summer institutes. And, of course, James Edie retains his impact upon the movement through work in the philosophy of language.

What I wish to point out here, however, is that there is a pattern which, in addition to the negative characterization which disclaims this work as either the mere exposition, repretition or extension of the masters, carries its own distinction. There are two characteristics which stand out: first, almost without exception, the American phenomenologists develop work which has *interdisciplinary* impact. There are at least two reasons for this. In the first place, phenomenology does not have its own subject matter. As a style of inquiry it is always "phenomenology of _____ ," with the blank to be filled in. The cases above illustrate the essentially interdisciplinary thrust of phenomenology. There is also a probable historical reason for this tendency as well. Given the at least earlier hostility of AE dominated departments, ACE philosophers frequently had to turn elsewhere for their audiences. Naturally, those disciplines which have surface similarities to phenomenology attracted multiple thinkers. Thus, were one to turn to psychology, the list of ACE eminents would be quite large (one thinks of Charles Scott, Amedeo Georgi, Robert Romanyshn and many others). Or, again in relation to the arts and literature, yet another set of names comes to mind (Arnold Berleant and Karsten Harries, to name just two).

Second, even beyond the outward glance of interdisciplinarity, these philosophers choose what might appear to be unusual, or at least untapped areas of inquiry. They explore less or even unexplored fields. Thus, in addition to silence, already mentioned, one finds an Alfonso Lingis dealing with cultural variations (including "savages" and "sepuku"). The same two reasons dealing with the essentially investigatory nature of phenomenology and the need to find untapped areas applies to this characteristic of American phenomenology.

And while I find this both fresh and intellectually exciting, it also continues to violate yet another secondary style characteristic of AE practice. The scientific paradigm, in what Kuhn would characterize as its *normal* phase, is one which concentrates upon a narrow set of problems and reworks these. Thus in analytic philosophy one finds, for example, countless articles on "Gettier Problems," decades of work on "reference" or "rigid designators." Not new fields to plow, but the retilling of the same soil over and over is what is preferred. While neither task is to be demeaned, functionally this difference of philosophical praxis is one reason (or excuse) why there remains a problem for philosophical visibility for ACE philosophers to AE philosophers. But here the tables must also be turned, because it could be that this invisibility remains the social practice of the aforementioned hygiene.

An interesting clue is again provided by citation patterns and the observation of the meeting practices of philosophers. A closer look at citations—except in the cases of giants of any traditions—reveals that not only do AE middleweights frequently cite each other within the argumentative paradigm, but this set of citations frequently constitutes the *only* set of citations. Contrarily, most of the well cited ACE philosophers draw their notability from a range of disciplines, primarily the humanities and the social sciences. They have a different ratio of visibility and invisibility. Visibility is outward as much or more than inward for ACE.

The same phenomena could be observed for many years of this period at the annual Eastern Division meetings of the APA. The sections of the central program—again excepting giants or darlings—could be seen to have very small attendance, in frequent contrast to the meetings of the special interest societies which were equally frequently overflowing. This imbalance made the profession look as if it was in danger of imploding. These observations, however, only confirm in a different way the perceptions of many outside philosophy, that there are many departments whose habits effectively isolate them from the larger intellectual life of universities.

Even if many in the center of the profession remained for a long time unconcerned with this phenomenon, publishers and others were not. The proliferation of Continental series attests to the wider reading public concerned with the *issues* discussed by ACE thinkers. Nor is this a matter of mere numbers or popularization—it has always struck me as ironic that a constant AE criticism of Continental philosophy has been its purported difficult language, terminology or jargon. Yet the wider and interdisciplinary audiences seem to have little problem with it.

In spite of the past intraphilosophical invisibility between AE and ACE, there has occurred a significant growth to the professional presence of a wide range of American Continentally oriented philosophers. This is particularly the case when newly tilled land draws attention, which it does with more frequency than those who keep their eye to one plow would like.

I am not claiming here more virtue on one side of the Rortean split than the other. If too many AE philosophers remain "hygenic" in their reading habits, it may be that too many ACE philosophers find their own consoling isolation in the esoterica of certain kinds of scholarship. But if I am right about a newly emergent maturity from within the now first generations of ACE, at least middleweights, then the directions which look outward, which explore new territory, and which pose new perspectives show a genuine health within precisely a no longer invisible community.

I have the dilemna here, to return in a different way in the last chapter. I am quite cognizant that by cutting off the discussion at this point I have left unmentioned the even larger generations of ACE philosophers who come from the decades of the forties and even fifties birthyears. But what I have traced is a history with a different profile than that found in Rorty's version of the Analytic-Continental split.

In the chapters to follow, which are simply examples of some of my own attempts to follow consequences of phenomenology, it will be seen that I, too, have work habits similar to my peers. There are traditional scholarly pieces (chapters seven and eight, on Ortega and Ricoeur); attempts to work through philosophical problems via confrontation with giants (chapters two and three on perception via Merleau-Ponty and Foucault and texts via Gadamer and Derrida); forays into little explored territory (chapter one on sounds and voice); and extensions into interdisciplinary regions (chapters four through six on technology). In that regard I continue to situate myself within the philosophical community of American Continental philosophers, but open to the plurality of positions in this diverse continent.

Part I
Perceptual
Polymorphy

Chapter 1

A Phenomenology of Voice

In the beginning was voice and the voice was speech and speech was Language. That is the case with the realm we call human, not that we are entirely different from the animals of the kingdom who are as perceptually immersed in the world as we. We can recognize the cat as she focuses her attention upon the morning squirrel, selecting this particular creature out of the vast complexity of the background of other beings and events. The cat evidently has those gestalts and figure/ground relationships which structure its world as ours.

Yet even in our perceptions, we find a lurking persistence of meaning which simultaneously involves and distances us from our immediate environment. For us to observe the cat watch the squirrel is to have placed both in a familiarly placed context, with names which give us Adamic power over them. Our language, however, is itself perceptually situated, embodied in receptive and expressive senses and bound to this primordial attachment to the world.

So, with language there is nothing without its concrete perceptual dimension. It is first heard, then spoken. The infant, even in the womb, hears the voices of language. Just as we—if we attend to it—feel our voices when we speak, resonate and cadence within our torso, so the infant feels the voice of language before it is thrust into the lighted world. Expressions of anger, of soothing song, and the familiarizing drone of daily speech is part of the memory of that time before distance. The voices of language are heard before spoken.

27

Language which is in speech which is in voice is that sounded center that our imaginations reach beyond the familiar. It is possible for us to imagine the first expression: a call, a scream, a yelp of delight, a nascent song, but even the first word is imagined from the unspoken and taken-for-granted center of already meaningful Language. We can no more pretend to imagine the fullness of a bare perceptual world prior to speech than we can imagine the non-existent dimension of light and dark which structures the blind person's experiences. (The "darkness" of the blind is as metaphorical as is his use of "I see you" while touching my face. It is a language without reference. It would be as easy for us to fulfill an imagination of the infrared spectrum seen by the bee as to imagine the total absence of light/dark in blindness.)

But a perception steeped in Language poses a problem for us which we may not even recognize. For it is a perception which is always too quick to make familiar the most strange and other which we come upon in the world. Perhaps only for moments do we come face to face with that which is truly other, and then we give it a name, domesticating it into our constant interpretation which centers us in the world.

I experienced such a novel event when I first heard the recorded sounds of the humpback whale. For the first moment the marvellous range and pattern of the whale voice presented the unique, never-before-heard. But too soon I began to bring this "song" into the familiarity, first of metaphor, then of name. I analogized the whale's voice such that its low notes were "like" those of a bellowing bull, its high notes "like" the shrill of a bird, etc. This had also already been done in that the dust cover of the record proclaimed it as whalesongs. In so doing the strangeness becomes domesticated.

Naming, however, is not neutral and our metaphors serve both to identify and guide, but also to take in certain rather than other directions. The biologist who named the utterance of the whale "singing," clearly had the metaphor of bird song in mind. But is even the song of a bird a song? If what we claim we know of the bird is correct, that its voices are those of territorial proclamation, of courting, of warning and calling, then the song is both like the opera with its melodrama and unlike the opera. For the melodrama of opera is acted, and song, even improvised, is a species of acting—but the bird is immersed in an acting which is simultaneously its very life. Even its vocal posturing has real effect.

What does the whale do? Does he sing like a bird, or like the old operatic whale, sing of Figaro? Or does he speak the voices of language and communicate with his kind? Or all of these? There remains an essential mystery to the voice of the whale, a mystery which we have not yet fully entered, but which we might forget if we simply allow the whale's voice to be domesticated as singing.

Our language/perception, a single phenomenon, is simultaneously that which involves us and distances us from the voices of the world. On the one side, it allows us to bring close the voices of the world, into a familiarity which identifies and structures our expectations. We "know" what to expect—just as the Rousseauan inclined anthropologist can be inclined to find the noble savage, or the Augustinian inclined anthropologist the instance of original sin—we, too, at the instant of identifying, know what to expect. Perhaps only rarely do we find ourselves shaken in our predispositions, such that the other breaks through in the voices of the world.

This strangeness can, however, break through even that which is presumably familiar. Religious chanting takes many forms and most persons recognize its forms immediately. But in the case of certain Tibetan chants a new and different phenomenon occurs. In its rhythmic and even repetitive movements the chant moves from monophonic to harmonic expressions, and lacking the presence of the monks, we are perhaps led to assume with our usual predisposition that the harmonic expressions are those of the choir—whereas in fact the polyphony is the voice of a single monk and the monophony that of the choir.

The Tibetan chant inverts what we ordinarily expect. It is an auditory figure/ground reversal, but a reversal which is quite typical of certain Eastern values. The same phenomenon occurs in certain kinds of Japanese paintings. What stands out as a single branch, often somewhat abstractly or expressionistically sketched, we might well take as the figure against the vague and indistinct ground of the background. But the seeing which is called for is to see the figure only as that which sets off the true subject of the painting, the Open, or the ground itself. The background is what is focal in this inversion.

Here we reach, however, a phenomenon well known to phenomenologists, the phenomenon of multistable possibilities, simultaneously open yet structured. In the early days of radio, Georg von Békésy discovered such a multistability in the ways in which the first listeners heard music through earphones. Some heard the music as if it were in front of them; others heard the music in a 180° reversal, as if it were coming from in back of them; and still others heard it "in the middle of their heads." Here were three different possible stabilities.

These possibilities are related to the double spatial presence of sound which we ordinarily experience when listening to music. To hear music is to simultaneously experience it both as directional and as atmospheric. It comes from a "there"—perhaps from the orchestra in front of us if at a live performance, *and* it surrounds us as a musical atmosphere in which we feel immersed. In the instrumental transformation of these two dimensions, the multistability of different possible direction occur.

The same multistability may be illustrated visually in this simple line drawing:

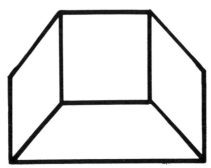

This visual phenomenon is one of the well known reversible drawings. For example, it may be seen as a "hallway" in which the central configuration is seen as a "rearward" appearing (and the viewer downward as it were from its position). Or, it may be seen as a topless pyramid with the central configuration upward or forward facing (and the viewer now elevated into a more birdseye apparent position). But this bistability does not exhaust the figure, since it can also be seen two-dimensionally. This time it is a "headless robot" which is standing directly upright, coming toward you, with the central configuration its body, the lines to the sides its arms and legs, and the uprights crutches upon which it holds its headless body.

Now in both the auditory and the visual version of multistability, we may note that each possibility is one which can actually be experienced in a certain way, but while so experienced the other possibilities equally there to be discovered are not experienced. There is an alternation of profiles or possibilities, but all belong to the structure of possibility exemplified by these phenomena.

What I have been suggesting is that our language/ perception overall functions in this way. In language each name, each metaphor allows us, if it is appropriate, to situate that which we experience in a certain way. But it is possible for this guidance, which is in some way essential to perceiving itself to be sedimented, fixed. It is possible that without the new metaphor, the "headless robot" might have been missed. It is possible that one might see only a hallway perpetually, because in each case there is a genuineness to that experience. But, once having begun the exercise of reversals and having opened the question of possibility, one begins to suspect that there are depths not yet plumbed.

Artists and phenomenologists share a certain practice, the practice of exploring the possible and of doing it in variant ways. Phenomenologists name this practice: it is the exploration of variations in order to discover invariants or structures. It is the purposeful reversal of figure/ground. It is the extension from figure to field to horizon, and so forth. But artists practice the same arcane path, for they show us reversals and deconstruct our metaphors, and in so doing, construct new ones with new perspectives. In music John Cage has frequently done this. By performing silence, he inverts the usual, the expected, and the multistability which occurs may be focused either on the silence itself, or upon the incidental sounds which occur and now become the "music."

Each new variation, each new metaphor, holds exploratory significance—but with a qualification, it must be seen to be only a variation, for the phenomenon itself doubtless hides more yet to be found. It is with this forewarning that I turn more precisely to the task here: a phenomenology of voice.

Voice is, for us humans, a very central phenomenon. It bears our language without which we would perceive differently. Yet outward from this center, voice may also be a perspective, a metaphor, by which we understand part of the world itself. For metaphor is to language what perspective is to perception, and both are integral to the way in which we experience things.

Languages in miniature—metaphors—are ways of seeing, of hearing. Aesthetics teaches us that perhaps better than most disciplines. It now seems strange to us that prior to the nineteenth century in the West, mountains were not often seen as beautiful, but rather as threatening, as blocking, as foreboding, until the landscapists domesticated them and made them objects of beauty. Or, take the now seemingly silly practice of the nineteenth century in which framing landscapes became a passion, with travellers regularly looking at the scenery through an oblong wire frame, thereby creating a framed, picture-like landscape. But perhaps this is little different than our contemporary artists who now go about draping coastlines and islands in plastic, thereby transforming the landscape into a kind of art object.

Similarly in music, the contemporary introduction of noise to be taken as music, of random sounds, of monotonous sounds, all strain at making a new gestalt for listening. This is artistic playfulness which the phenomenologist can also appreciate. And my first move beyond this setting of context is to do similar variations with the idea of voice.

What if we take voice—which in a narrow sense is distinctively human—and first expand it as a metaphorical perspective, following a suggestion of Merleau-Ponty who spoke of the "voices of silence," and of "singing the world." The metaphor is serious and not frivolous, for there is a deep sense in which all things, the things of the world, have voices. We miss this because of at least two things: first, we exist in a language world which is frequently dominated by visualism. Thus often perception itself is reduced to the visual. This does not mean that I wish to substitute a different sense as model here, because I do not more wish to simply reduce the visual than to simply enhance the auditory. What I am trying to do is to demonstrate the sedimentation which is reductive, reductive of both the visual and the auditory.

The first set of voices I wish to point out are those of material things. For every material thing has a voice—which, however, is all too easy to miss. First, we may miss the voices of things because they are often, left by themselves, mute or *silent*. We recognize this when the silence is dramatic and overpowering. The city dweller who for the first time finds himself or herself in a desert might think the desert silent by contrast—but this silence is only relative in that a careful listening would hear the heat crackle of the sand, the small sounds of insect life, and perhaps the slight voice of the wind.

But individual things might well remain silent, their voices not active. Yet each thing can be given a voice. The rock struck, sounds in a voice; the footstep in the sand speaks muffled sound. Here, however, we must note that the voices of things which are often silent are made to sound only in duets or more complex polyphonies. When I strike a lecturn you hear both the voice of the lecturn and of my knuckle. When I use a pen to strike the water pitcher, you hear both the sound of the glass and of the plastic, simultaneously in a duet of voices of things.

Here we must attend carefully to our perception. For to isolate the voice of a thing, we must listen carefully and focus upon one of the voices in the duet. We can do this in making one of the voices focal—the auditory figure as it were—and the other background. If we listen to a quartet of instruments, we can select out the clarinet to attend to even while the oboe continues to play simultaneously. And to listen to one voice of a duet is what we must do if we are to hear distinctly what is said in the voices of things.

And what do we hear? The answer is much, for the voices of things bespeak the multiple dimensions of the thing. For example, the thing bespeaks something of its material nature in its sounding. The solidity of the table is bespoken when it sounds, even in some cases telling us of its kind of materiality. The wooden table sounds differently than the metal table. The brass goblet bespeaks differently than the glass goblet. Each bespeaks something of its nature. Moreover, it cannot do otherwise.

More, it also bespeaks something of its shape and dimension. The voices of things often tell of interiors. By tapping on a wall, I can hear whether it is solid or has a hollow behind it. By striking the barrel, I can tell whether is contains only air, or is filled with some liquid—or even if it is but partially filled. Interiors sound. They are bespoken in the voices of things.

Or, I may take the voices of things and let them reverberate so that I can tell something even about that which remains silent. For example, if I strike something in a large auditorium, the space which is auditorily given to me is distinctly different than the space given by striking the same object in a closet. And again it is different if I am in a room with bare walls and hard floors, than in a room filled with drapes and rugs. In short, our listening experiences a complex and multidimensioned richness of things which sound, but which we rarely attend to with deeper attention than ordinary consciousness.

The same occurs in the voices of nature, where at least a duet is heard in the wind and trees, but more often a multiplicity of voices sound at once, thereby making the isolation of singlenesses difficult and thereby precluding the tendency to discrete isolations. This community of sound, this multiplicity of voices is also frequent in the natural world. The multiple voices of waves, wind and sand constantly sound the multiplicity of voices of the things of nature.

All this is to say that the sound of voices taken in this sense is constant and complex. So long as we are conscious there is a sounding world (similarly, visually, even when we close our eyes, we see—the darkness of our closed eyes, or the faint glow of bright lights through our lids.) If the voices are taken as a kind of music, it varies in place to place and time to time from pianissimo to forte, from a few voices to many, but it is never totally silent. And the most silent of the things of the world, can be given sounding voices in the duets of contact and motion.

Taken in this way, we invert the usual relation of music to the field of sound, for there is a fundamental sense in which the sounds of the world are the first music, with what we call music in a narrower sense as a kind of abstracting from this auditory realm, perhaps setting it in an auditory frame, perhaps enhancing and embroidering upon it. So, in a kind of ironic turn, by taking the world as voice and music, we come to see what we ordinarily take as voice and music is a particular configuration within the world of sound.

And there is more that we can discover in this phenomenological playing at the edge of artistic practice. The contemporary penchant to change perspectives may also be seen to fit here. Insofar as any thing can be given a voice, it can become an instrument. Thus the musician who takes the world this way, may play the things of the world as instruments, improvising among the voices of things. The street urchin who runs a stick along the picket fence, or who drums a rhythm out of garbage cans, is giving voices and even a kind of music to the things of the world. "High" or "fine" art is in this sense but a refinement of possibilities discovered in the voices of things. The things of the world are thus instruments as well and anything can be an instrument, made to sound, to give voice.

The voices of things are not the voices of language. For what the voices of things bespeak is a kind of direct sound of their natures: materiality, density, interiority, relations within experienced space, outward hollows and shapes; complex, multidimensioned, often unheard in potential richness, but spoken in the voices of things.

When we reach the kingdom of animal voices, however, we reach the neighborhood of language. For here expression begins to occur, expression of more than material nature, expression of action and emotion. First note that the voices which begin to be expressive are communitarian in voice. Many creatures in the animal world behave more like choirs than individuals in conversation. The coyote who begins to bay at the moon is not long in solo, but soon is joined in choir. Geese in flight honk in a virtual cacaphony. The baboon troup does not fret itself about who interrupts whom, for all chatter while on trek. And there is expression in these voices. Who can mistake the contentedness of the purr of the domestic cat, the excitement and genuine joy of the dog whose master returns? The range from whimper to the distinctive sounds animal owners recognize for food, for strangers, for warnings, for other animals show the expressivity of the voices of the animals. Take, too, the mimics. There is unintended visual mimicry: the viceroy butterfly mimics its larger, presumably ill tasting monarch in pattern, color and design. But the mocking bird, parrot, and cockatoo all consciously imitate and mimic the voices of others. Here is an expression doubled upon itself, the wedge in sound which opens the way to what becomes in the voices of language the complexity of the ironic, the sarcastic, the humorous and all the multidimensionality of human speech, particularly in its dramaturgical form.

Although I shall not explore all the possibilities of animal communication I think it should be obvious that in speaking of voice here, if not yet of the voices of language, we are leaving the sense of metaphor and entering the neighborhood of voice at its center. Although—if there is an animal vocabulary—it may be narrower, and if "language," less rich and transparent, the possibilities of expression are already beginning to open. For with animals as with humans, voice is an active expressing of relations with others and the environment. Voice changes the way we so relate and frees us from the limited territory of the unuttered. There is a kind of auditory migration which begins with voice, even in the kingdom of animals.

Animal voices usually remain close to that which we discovered in the voices of things. This is especially the case with spatial significations. Calls tell where the speaker is as both part of the communication and as directly heard. And there is a vestigial sense in which the voice of the animal bespeaks its nature. The birdwatcher, without looking, awakes to the calls which are those *of* the bluejay, the white throated sparrow, the grackle. But in another sense the material nature of the animal is now often belied. For the smaller creature may speak with a louder voice than the larger. And with the arrival at both mimicry and the active posturing which expressivity allows, the voices of animals begin to open to the dramaturgical. The gorilla's visual (chest pounding) and auditory (roaring) gestures are simultaneously posturing and actions, creating the aura which is distinctively gorillian.

Animal voices, too, serve as musical material. One movement in the West was obviously outward from voice to instrument, with early instruments as quasimimics of voice. But animal voices are also that from which a music can begin. The sounds of primitive flutes, particularly in Andean music, are birdlike and bird song often is the theme around which the music takes shape.

I have been moving from outward back toward the center, the voices of language, which are the position from which we experience the world. I have suggested that precisely because this is where we live and breathe and transform breath into more than breath, into voiced speech, that we have difficulty understanding this center. So given as this center is, so familiar and taken-for-granted, and for precisely that reason so opaque, it is not without reason that we humans have turned to often fruitless speculations about the origins of language.

In philosophy the question of language has been the preoccupation of the twentieth century. This is the case both in the dominant Anglo-American analytic traditions and with the Continental traditions. And each tell a different story. On the one side the tale is told of an origin in descriptive naming: the first word of language is predicating a "literal" description to some existent object. S is some kind of P. The other tribe tells a different tale: the first word is a kind of metaphor which may be a primitive kind of expression, but one with multiple significations. And between these tribes arises a warfare in which the one claims that the multiple (the metaphor) is a built up complexity out of simples; while the other claims that the simples are "dead metaphors" reduced from rich original expression of an original word.

But these tales of origin, like the myths which every human group has about beginnings, are, while imaginative and suggestive, ultimately fruitless. For we cannot find, return to, or isolate a first word. Even the mythology of the child is useless because members of one of these tribes will hear in the child's first word a name, which may be taken to mean one and only one thing; while the member of the other tribe will claim that the first word is something like all of language in a word, used in many ways until it diversifies as it does in learning. (But I would remind us of the earlier observation, that for the child, language is first heard, long before expressed, and thus whatever the first word is, it merely responds to the totality and complexity of the voices of language already familiar, acted upon and even in some sense understood.)

These origin speculations are not unlike speculations we might make about the first music. Was music made first by playing one note? A stick hit against a hollow tree? Or was it invented by the tribal singing which early humans, like their animal cousins, indulged in *en masse*? Obviously, we can never know which, if either, of these is the correct tale and we waste our best thought by pursuing such tales unless we realize they are but tales. For what we have are the already full voices of language and we find our center there.

And what of these voices? Are they one? Or many? Simple? Or complex? By avoiding the tales of origins, we are closer to a possible answer. For, whatever else the voices of language may be, at the center where we are, they are rich, multidimensioned and filled with as yet unexplored possibilities. But we should have expected that already from what we have noted about even the voices of things. The problem with the voices of things, below the level of expression and communication, is that too much is presented.

In bespeaking the possibilities of nature, of shapes, surfaces, interiors, surrounding spaces, there is too much "truth" as Merleau-Ponty observed. We have to interrogate with specific questions, specific actions, if we are to learn the possible lessons of the world. We do this, of course, without necessarily being fully aware of it. For example, we actually rather constantly "echo locate" as we now call auditory spatial orientation. Sometimes I conduct an experience experiment with my students to show this. I take them into an unobstructed and hard-walled corridor and draw a chalk mark down the hall and tell them to walk to it; turn around; and return to the original starting point. In doing this I ask them to attend carefully to the sounds of their shoes as they echo against the walls, opening the way to the variants they are about to undergo.

Then I have them put on a good set of ear mufflers (mine is a set which I use in chain sawing, like those which airline workers use near jet planes). These mufflers, while not closing off the world of sound, do muffle it sufficiently to dramatically demonstrate what we would experience without echo location. It is at first a rather irreal experience in which the solidity of the floor even seems muted. And one obviously has to sharpen his or her visual attentiveness to the task at hand. Then, I have them put on a blindfold instead of the ear muffler and perform the same task, now more aware of the role of echo location. And, interestingly, few fail to do a right approach and most report that they can now hear the distance from the two walls since they are now attending to what they had all along done without noticing, but now notice more fully. This, in short, is a sharpened question put to the world. In the last variation, the student tries with both blindfold and muffler and in this case, almost invariably, the wall is soon encountered. Our spatial orientation is not and never has been simply visual—yet we have often so interpreted it.

Now the reason I returned to this voiced spatiality of things here is to suggest that we may be as badly off in our usual interpretation of the voices of language as we have been in our interpretation of experienced spatiality. And, if we are to begin to probe the multidimensionality of voice, we will have to pay subtle attention to it at its most dramatic point. That is why, I shall turn to what I call *dramaturgical* voice.

Human voice recapitulates what we have previously noted. Even from the world of things, voice retains vestigially some sense of the materiality we are. Sometimes, and against the will of the speaker, what is spoken is not desired. The wheezing voice of the emphysemiac, of the too far along smoker, bespeaks the interior state of the body and its pathology. More mundanely, the spatial significations of where, of direction, and of surroundings are also sounded. The playful hollering to catch echoes in the mountains is a variant of the sounding of surrounding space we found a possibility of things.

But as the realm of animals in the neighborhood of language reveals, expressivity is not only of material nature, but of expressivity. Not only the where of speech, as in a call, is presented, but the *who* of voice. The distinctiveness of voice, even transformed over the telephone, is recognizable. And in this recognition we have a phenomenon which is probably known also in the animal realm. The "who speaks" is never auditorily only a where, nor of simple distinctive pattern. It is also musical in that musical sound enhances the directionality and the atmospheric dimensions of sound. So with voice: one's voice is simultaneously there, and it is a kind of surrounding. It presents us with an auditory atmosphere, an auditory aura. The self-aware dramaturgical speaker knows this and enhances this phenomenon. The actor's ability to project, the orator to enhance resonances, thereby enhances the aura of dramatic presence.

With expressivity, the doubling of significance is also possible. Mimicry, perhaps the simplest doubling, is elaborated in the human realm by all manner of doubling. Irony, sarcasm, duplicity, and even lying become possibilities, as well as humour, double entendre and wit. All of this is expressed vocally, auditorily.

All speech is dramaturgical in a significant sense. This is

not to say that there is not good or bad, appropriate and inappropriate dramaturgy. Amongst my tribe—the philosophers—there is a notorious and sometimes even highly valued amount of "bad" dramaturgy. A technical, detailed and better-read-than-said paper, read dryly and monotonously at a professional meeting is not undramaturgical. It often "says" far more than it intends and the dominance of this kind of speech probably is one factor in the decline of undergraduate interest in philosophy in recent times. But it is its own kind of dramaturgy—a kind of dramaturgy which tries to deny itself. The "truth" is not to be found, so says the tribe, in the way it is expressed. But this is to mistake the possibility that the "truth" might just as easily be discovered in the felicitous and well voiced expression as in the dullest.

The multidimensioned possibilities of dramaturgical voice, however, also exceed the dimension of mere expression. Dramaturgical voice reveals a world. Here we reach the voices of language. For through the voice, a world is presented. And with it a curious thing happens. The very voice which at its height of good dramaturgy, simultaneously draws attention to itself, and yet denies itself on behalf of the world which is presented.

This is what the poet does. Poetry (which in our examples may be assumed to be read aloud) does draw attention to the language, to voiced language. There is a beauty to the words themselves, the cadences and rhythms of the poem. But there is more, for *through* the voice of language in the poem, a world or a new perspective on the world is heard.

What lies within these voices, central to the very way we experience world, is almost too complex to deal with. For much is said in even the single expression. Here, however, what is voiced, sounded, is our focus. For the sound of voice already bespeaks much. The modulations which are sounded, we already know, for even a word is multiple in its auditory context and if I address you as:

> You!
> You?
> You.

I have already voiced three different possibilities of the voices of language. And I have done so in the economy of voice, situated as it is in the unspoken but understood field of language. This silence, this unspoken background to the foreground of my words is also part of the voice of language.

Every dimension of spoken voice, carefully heard, presents a multiple dimensioned wealth. This is particularly apparent in purposeful dramaturgical voice. Even the "who" of speech is multiple. This phenomenon is probably most familiar in the voice of the actor or the singer. On stage or in cinema, Richard Burton plays a role and in the role there are two voices which synthesize. The Hamlet he plays is vocally animated out of the drama, yet it is Burton's Hamlet. The Pavorotti who sings the Duke in "Il Trovatore" is both Duke and Pavorotti. Here is a recapitulated set of dimensions which range from the unmistakable "nature" of individual voice to the exhibited voice of another.

This same possibility is taken even further in the dramaturgy of liturgical voice, for in the more extreme cases, the voice of the cantor, the priest, the liturgist is disguised and amplified within the echoing space of the cathedral, synagogue or temple, so that the voices of the gods may once again be heard. Again, an extreme example of such a voice one may again recall the Temple chant of the Tibetans. Those who sing-chant the polyphonous voice of the sacred, are selected at childhood for lifelong training, so that the dramaturgy of their voices can be the voices of the gods.

What dramaturgical voice presents is the multidimensioned and multipossibilitied phenomenon of voice. The voices of language, display for us a range of possible worlds, themselves multidimensional. And the voices of the speakers also double and redouble throughout the range of possibilities. This is the primary phenomenon. But it is not all. For although all language is embodied, and it is first embodied in sound, heard and then spoken, it also has become differentiated in such a way that voice no longer stands alone as that perceptual-linguistic way of experiencing the world.

I refer to writing as a visual embodiment of language. For sometime in a past no longer remembered, sound became at first related to letter, and then submerged in writing in the modern sense in seen, but unsounded words. This momentous gestalt shift, now taken for granted, was probably itself gradual.

Briefly take note of a few overlappings in this emergence

of a different embodiment of language. Early reading was apparently habitually reading out loud. The student who discovered Ambrose reading silently, without even moving lips, was witness to a profound change and separation within the realm of language in a visual embodiment. This later development has become so much the case that today we are often surprised when we pick up a book, written by a friend, and hear in our reading his or her voice.

Today, again within the tribes of philosophers, the phenomenon of writing has become a preoccupation. This is particularly the case with the contemporary and primarily French post-structuralist traditions. Derrida proclaims, extremely, that writing actually precedes speech in the form of inscription and "trace." Lyotard speaks of a writing which writes itself. And in the focus upon writing, the deconstruction of the self occurs—for writing can hide a self far better than voice which always carries within itself that recapitulation of voiced self.

Moreover, the emergence and evolution of writing has today led to an even more extreme set of possibilities, unvoicable writing or "language." Here I refer to symbolic or constructed languages, those of symbolic logic, of mathematics and of computer symbols. Language no longer voiced. Given this possibility, voice may be forgotten, covered over. This effect, I would contend, may be detected in a number of disciplines which relate both directly and indirectly to the auditory realm.

A few examples: Phonetics, which is presumably the discipline which deals with sounded words, in effect reduces spoken language to a kind of code of letters—translates sounds into the units we may call broadly, letters. The phonetic alphabet, a shorthand for discrete sounds, is a set of letters for sounds. Thus phonetics, not unlike the latent visualism in most of our science, learns what it learns by first translating an auditory realm into a visual one.

The same happens with attempts to learn speech patterns by playing them upon an oscillograph. Again, what is sounded is translated to a visual pattern. Distinctive voice "signatures" perfectly well recognized in a listening gestalt, now may be made to "stand" on the photographed pattern and taken account of visually. We can then repeat and make stand still the utterance. These are all attempts, often successful, to reduce and translate auditory to visual forms.

Here, however, we place ourselves at a crucial juncture, one which could take us in the wrong direction. For we are faced with the possibility of a Romantic nostalgia. We see this accelerated translation of auditory to visual and in it—surely—there lurks the possibility of a "reduction" of the auditory and of a forgetfulness of its richness. And I do not deny that this is possible. But if, then, we decry the now doubled presence of perception/language in this auditory/visual, we place ourselves in a similar role which is to merely reassert another privilege.

Too much is gained, genuinely, in the new variation. And the sciences of phonetics, linguistics and the advances of literacy are too vast to simply dismiss or reject. If, in the new visual, that is not the greatest danger. The greatest danger is the second reduction which reduces both sound and sight to such notions as "information"—as if the only thing conveyed in speech and writing is what the technology proclaims.

The forgetfulness which is possible, is always at most a partial and particular forgetfulness. At its worst, it can cause us to overlook and to become insensitive to the full richness and range of the auditory. And it can take us in certain, rather than other directions. In music, for example, the introduction of writing is the introduction of notation. Notation does for music what writing does for language. For example, it allows repetition. While every performance is different, every inter-pretation different, a core signification remains discernible and Beethoven's Fifth remains his Fifth just as Burton's Hamlet remains Shakespeare's Hamlet.

Such a tradition, now deeply engrained in our practices, is essentially different from music in oral traditions (which are in a sense now hard to find). In recent times, through tape recording folk music, particularly, in isolated rural areas of the world, we have discovered that even the notion of the "same" is different in oral compared to literate cultures. The "same" song, particularly if it is one with many verses and complex, will on the tape both be different through time with a single singer, and different with different performers—yet both will proclaim that they have sung the same song. Here the core persistent significance of the song is not that *literal* repetition of words and notes which it might be for the literate culture, but the pattern, the overall sense of the song. "Sound" is not the letter, it is the spirit of the song.

This is not to say that either precision or excellence of performance is enhanced only in a tradition which follows notation. Rather, it is that a tradition of notation can enhance discreteness, strict repetition, reproduction. The same thing happens when we "read" time, as in clock cultures. All peoples have a sense of time, and we know that non-clock cultures (again hard to find) may be said metaphorically to have "read" time from the sun and moon and stars. But this is not true—such was not a reading and its results are different. To speak of "reading" in this sense is to anachronistically project our sensibility into another time and space.

But once having begun to read time with instruments the trajectory towards the discrete could begin. Clocks—even earlier the sundial and waterclock-represented time as an instant portrayed by the pointer moved. As clocks evolved, first from those which had only hour hands—to mark the hours of devotions—to those which then introduced minutes, then seconds, and now microseconds, the tendency towards enhancing the instant and to enhancing the discrete accelerated. So that today, with a digital clock, we no longer even represent the field of time in which the instant occurs. In this we not only change a perception of time, we also reduce its dimensions in our representations. What we gain in discreteness, we lose in expanse.

My point here is this: different embodiments entail different selectivities. The same applies to speech and writing. And within the same realm, the same applies even to differences such as those which scored compared to improvised musical performances display. The variations display differences. In speech there is an economy which is possible in expression. The here-and-now perceived context, while unspoken is apparent in the communication situation. And the multidimensionality of the expression can, in even short phrases, say much. Thus the scream of "Fire," in a crowded theatre carries with it the experienced context, the sense of urgency heard in the sounding of the voice, and the alarm and imperative of the word. To deal with the same in the representativeness of writing—it would not mean the same nor even make the same sense were the word, "fire," simply written on a page—one must write out the context which, if skilled might still be economical, but clearly not in the same sense as the voiced situation.

Contrarily, writing can preserve and enrich the sense of that which is *not* here and now. I would never have learned of my father's crude poetic abilities had I not discovered a package of old love letters between him and my mother while cleaning out the homestead for sale this fall. There is a different gain and a different loss in each of the embodiments of language. And these gains can then be translated positively, as well as negatively. For where the alphabet of phonetics clearly *loses* the individual and dramaturgical sound of a voice in its translation, in the new version of "auditory writing"—I refer to the tape recording—we capture, like writing, what was past and that which can be repeated just as a book is reread.

Central to what I have been saying is the notion of a perceptual multistability. What is deeper, and what is richer, is discovered through the process of variations. To understand more adequately the ambiguous drawing, the reversibilities of figure/ground in aesthetics, is to begin to probe the very structures of possibility. That has always been the phenomenological task, and in practice it is also the artistic task.

The same applies to what may have appeared just now as a kind of detour. For voice, in the human dimension inextricably linked to perception/language, encounters in its history a new perception/language in writing. Each are what I have called embodiments of Language, but each carries its own kind of distinctive stability. And each kind of stability has its temptation to reduction, but also the possibility of enrichment.

When we return from this detour, however, we also reach a juncture with respect to that other human expressivity in sound: music. Clearly, notation is for music what writing is for the linguistic. Yet with a difference—for while writing may gradually separate itself from voice and sound, for notation to become an end in itself without music, is to transform something beyond its horizon. Thus with notation we reach a curious dialectic. Could music be reduced to the unsounded? translated entirely into the visual? (If so, we should at least be hesitant to call it music except as metaphorical. Indeed, it might be more a dance.) Insofar as music must remain sounded, it is not its score. Yet with notation, music may be performed in ways which exceed the bounds of purely oral tradition. This, of course, is merely to have rediscovered the very history of our music. It is a music, which through the score, is repeatable, controllable, and now embodied in recording technologies, distributable as an auditory library for anyone.

Yet, music also exceeds its notation. And today this seems apparent in the very way in which notation itself must change to accommodate what is sounded. New sounds, no longer bound to the scales and conventions of the past, call for new notations—the symbolic logics of contemporary music. But this is the interplay between the dimensions of the languages of sight and voice which could be mutually enriching.

What I am suggesting comes directly from what I would term a phenomenological insight. The discipline which takes the structure and field of possibility as its theme, is the discipline which finally arrives at the notion of a multi-dimensioned, multistable field as the central model of the world. And what I am implying has at least heuristic value. Negatively, this implies that romanticism can be as reductive as other possible moves.

We noted in the multistable visual figure at least three possibilities: the "hallway," the "pyramid" and the "headless robot." Each was an equivalent possibility and one replaces the other in the procession of profiles. But by doing the variations—not even yet exhaustive—we also did something else. We ascended to a beginning insight into the very structure of multistability, an insight which then can guide our subsequent awareness, such that we might well expect both more possibilities and, in other similar drawings, the same multiplicity of profiles.

I am intimating that the same thing happens in the action of language/perception and that the voices of language are a stability which have become supplemented by the writings of language. Reduced to a mere speaking-hearing being (naturally an impossibility even to concretely imagine), or similarly reduced to a mere seeing-seen being, we would clearly experience the world in a flat and reduced way. We are multisensory and have always been so. Interestingly, we have not always explicitly been so as language/perceiving beings. Thus what I am suggesting is that the discovery and invention of writing in all its variations, is like the coming into sight of a blind man. The languages of vision, now exceeding the alphabet, enrich this connection with the world. They are variants upon the possibilities of multistability.

All the sound, we noted, is the field which might be called the field of possibilities for music, even as anything might be an instrument, and all voices primordial musical statements. Similarly, improvisation in at least one fundamental sense is primitive. Living is fundamentally improvisation. Without this, any new situation, could be destructive, because the world is constantly facing us with such situations. Yet, we also know that within the world not all strategies are successful. Thus at the animal as well as the human level, improvisation is always related to patterned actions.

Societies, cultures, which are oral ones, can be as restrictedly sedimented and patterned in repeated ways, as even the patterns of animal life display. Thus even the improvisation, the individual way in which traditional Armenian folk song begins with a display of the vocalists range, becomes part of the set pattern of the music.

The voices of language show us the same interplay. For whereas we may improvise an infinity of new sentences in an infinity of new situations, there would be no language without the stability of words, conventions, samenesses which while changing with time, do so in such a way that the letting-be-seen and letting-be-heard is Language in operation.

There is no return to a pure oral culture—or to pure spontaneity but what I am suggesting is that this is not a loss. A person who both hears and sees is better off than one blind or deaf; a language/perception embodied in spoken *and* in written articulations is better potentially than a single embodiment of significance. Yet within each of these dimensions and the range of multistability, there are those who will opt for the security of repetition and others who will opt for change. But he or she who discerns the possible, can "dance," (which is yet another language/perception and yet belongs to the gestalt which is human.) And, like Nietzsche, if I am to have any gods, I prefer those who dance in all the realms which we inhabit.

Chapter 2

Is There Always Perception?

Preface

Is there always perception? In this question there is a multiplicity of related concerns at different levels. In the simplest and most straightforward sense the question addresses an understanding of perception: if there is perception what does it include? what are its features? does it have an essential structure? Were one to be straightforwardly phenomenological, that could be the way in which the question is addressed. But within the broad frontiers which are known today as the Continental philosophies, it is no longer possible to raise questions in this direct way. This for two reasons: first, within this tradition it is apparent that the very notion of perception takes radically different meanings. And, second, the displacement of phenomenology particularly on the French scene by post-structuralist thought, poses a challenge to the very notion of perception. Thus I shall have to address the issues here obliquely and in such a way as to respond to three different levels of concern. I shall have to relocate the issue of perception in its contextual situation in the current debates. I shall have to account for the post-structuralist challenge to the notion and role of perception. And I shall have to reclaim for perception its role and philosophical significance for the present.

Perception and the Tradition

A first sketch of the differing notions of perception may be diachronic. Taking Husserl and Heidegger as our "classic" figures, we find that the discussion of perception exists in the context of both Modern (empiricist and rationalist) and transcendental (Kantian) forms. Husserl's approach to perception is the most conservative. While genuinely developing a first phenomenology of perception, he remains within the penumbra of Modern, particularly empiricist philosophy. This can be seen in the vestigial language which echoes the earlier traditions, language which includes the infamous "hyle," "noema," "sensation," and the like. It is as if perception could be built up of constituent parts, and although this language is used heuristically and rhetorically to introduce more radical concepts, Husserl fails to escape the nonneutral sedimented meanings of the earlier traditions.

Furthermore, Husserl's perceptual conservatism remains tied—as Heidegger so clearly showed—to an ontology of material objects. Thus even though the aim of the infamous *Fifth Meditation* of his *Cartesian Meditations* has a radically different purpose in uncovering our perceptions of others, it remains the case that his approach is one which takes as a primitive, a material body (or Cartesian object), to which is *appresented* the notion of a living self. The form of the analysis, if not its content, remains bound to the traditions of Modern philosophy.

Heidegger, as the other of our "classic" phenomenologists, is enigmatic with respect to perception. First, because he rarely mentions perception at all, except in the *Grundprobleme*, and, secondly, because of his sensitivity to the nonneutrality of sedimented meanings, he simply allows perception to be taken in a more Kantian representationalist sense and undercuts it. We are well enough aware in retrospect that part of the Heideggerian strategy with respect to perception relates to his ontology which is essentially different from the Husserlian one. Rather than a paradigm of a Modern philosophical observer noting material objects within which perception is central, Heidegger poses a theory of action. *Pragmata* are primary and whatever the material object is, it is derived from and is an abstraction from actional schema rather than material objects and with this displacement, perception too is shunted aside. Note that the *existentalia* of *Being and Time* do not include perception. Instead, *State-of-Mind*, *Understanding* and *Interpretation* are Dasein's "opening to the world." Perception is encompassed in a derivative position within understanding and interpretation.

In baldest terms, in Husserl we have a kind of neo-empiricist perceptualism vestigially tied to the observationalist framework of the Modern traditions where observer consciousness perceptually contemplates the realm of material objects. And in Heidegger, we have a kind of historicolinguistic theory of action, in which actional involvements take place in language contexts within which a world is revealed or made manifest. Yet in spite of this difference, there remains one set of deep sympathies with respect to the possibility of reclaiming the significance of perception.

This subterranean sympathy may be seen in what I shall term the concrete results of both Husserl's and Heidegger's analyses. With Husserl that result is at the very least the development of a *multidimensional* paradigm for perception. Husserl, in contrast to both the Modern and Kantian traditions, restores to the sense of the object, its "thickness" or "depths," by including within perception itself both what is manifest and what is latent, the "given" and the "meant." The object emerges from its earlier reduced sense as a composite of qualities or a bare surface and is expanded to the transcendent infinity of both presence and absence which becomes the paradigm for all subsequent phenomenological analysis. (Concretely, Husserl's die—a small cube—is always both given as a three-dimensional set of profiles before one *and* the infinity of meant, but concretely possible profiles which constitute the depth of the cube. Multidimensionality is found in this interplay of present and meant and in the location of the object in a field and in the notions of inner and outer horizons.) Multidimensionality becomes the paradigm for humanly possible perception.

This multidimensionality is not disputed by Heidegger. Indeed, it is taken for granted but displaced. It is, on one side, relocated in the progression of metaphysical sediments which he proposes to deconstruct. Thus in *Being and Time* the Cartesian "flat" view of the world is seen as a "covering over" of the richness of the actional world from which it is derived. Dasein is placed in the World and becomes concretely spatial in a description that clearly anticipates those of Merleau-Ponty. "Being-in" is clearly a multidimensional kind of existential spatiality from which the geometric abstractions of the Modern traditions can be seen to be reductions. However, this multidimensionality is not called perceptual by Heidegger—it is instead relocated within the progression of interpretations which constitute his hermeneutic method.

Already at the beginnings of phenomenology, one can see that perception is enigmatic, particularly with regard to strategies. But with the subsequent development of the inheritors of this tradition, perception becomes even more so. Here I switch from a diachronic scheme regarding ancestors, to a synchronic one in which one arranges positions along a continuum of extremes in which our ancestors, Husserl and Heidegger, occupy roughly middle positions.

One extreme, developed in part precisely because the ancestors make such a position possible, is taken by Merleau-Ponty. Like Husserl, Merleau-Ponty makes perception central. The primacy of perception is a theme which runs through his opus, although developed in different ways at different times. But his perception is not Husserl's. Instead, it may be described as simultaneously Husserl's and Heidegger's, as if Being-in-the-World is taken perceptualistically. Perception is the human concrete opening to the world and the base of knowledge and action. "The perceived world is the always presupposed foundation of all rationality, all value, all existence."[1] Merleau-Ponty's embodied, incarnate human is actional, like Dasein, but also centrally perceptual, as within a Husserlian trajectory. But perception now is broadened in scope to include much more than what was traditionally contained in either the micro-perception of sensation or of observer consciousness. All this is well enough known. But in this move—and it is part of what I wish to develop more precisely below—Merleau-Ponty makes another move which further radicalizes the notion of perception. To the multidimensionality of phenomenologically understood perception, he adds the notion of *multistability*. In the broadest sense this is the famed ambiguity of perception, but in a more precise sense, it is also the location of perception on a macrolevel in a more Heideggerian historicolinguistic context. Merleau-Ponty's best illustrations of this multi-stability come from aesthetics. One could, in fact, construct a progression of ways of seeing (multistabilities) from his aesthetic observations. This development is already present in

"The Primacy of Perception," where he observes, "It is a remarkable fact that the uninstructed have no awareness of perspective and that it took a long time and much reflection for men to become aware of the perspectival deformation of objects."[2] And to the late *Visible and Invisible* where he profoundly notes that "I say that the Renaissance perspective is a cultural fact, that perception itself is polymorphic and that if it became Euclidian, this is because it allows itself to be oriented by the system. What I maintain is that: there is an informing of perception by culture which enables us to say that culture is perceived."[3]

So far, phenomenology: but on our now synchronically extended continuum, I wish to place a new set of relatives, the post-structuralists who have made it necessary for us to even more radically resituate the question of perception. Perhaps the most enigmatic is our "boa-deconstructor," Derrida, who enigmatically proclaims that there never was perception. His position—which I shall not develop here—is derivative from Heidegger's. Rather than perception, what lies at the base of the changes of human understanding, are the progressions of writings, incarnate markings and inscriptions which even precede speech. "Perception," now in scarequotes is clearly a kind of historical invention which appears at a certain time and in a certain context. It—like the subject and even the world in post-structuralism—presumably disappears at some point in a coming set of perspective switches which constitute the *refractional paradigm* of deconstructionism.

Today, however, I wish to focus more upon another near relative, Michel Foucault. It is Foucault who most strongly attacks what he calls phenomenology, particularly in its Husserlian form. But his real rival is Merleau-Ponty.

Foucault, the former student of Merleau-Ponty, learned his lessons well. And with a subtlety not unlike that of Merleau-Ponty, he both parallels and attempts to outdo the master. *The Order of Things* Foucault begins with an analysis of Velázquez's painting, "Las Meninas." Then, from an exquisite analysis of representationalism self-reflected, he goes on to his chapter on "The Prose of the World." However, what is established in *The Order of Things* is, again, the refractive paradigm of post-structuralism.

Perception plays a different role in Foucault than in

Merleau-Ponty. It is placed in a semiotic matrix. Its role with respect to an environment becomes multistructural with different perceptions constituted variantly in different "epistemes." For Foucault, even "man" is but a historical occurrence and following what I am calling the refractional paradigm, what remains is the play of refractions—almost automated—to which we are historically tied. Yet the presumed disappearance of the "world" and the "self" (surrogate, I presume for all the possibilities of a subject, whether incarnate lived bodies, Dasein, or the ego cogito), there is an important philosophical issue which implicates perception.

Detour into Foucault

If one characterizes Foucault's archeological method of interpretation, what emerges is something like this: Each era in particularly western intellectual history is marked by the emergence of a set of structures and often hidden or unconsciously held assumptions which interdisciplinarily or cross-scientifically determine a set of practices which are followed. This "structure"—to use a scare-quoted term perhaps not quite amenable to Foucault—is clearly transsubjective, not invented by any individual, but nevertheless operates nearly universally in an epoch.

Foucault's method is also one which quite purposely inverts the values of what he takes to be the received or standard views of intellectual history. This view, he takes, emphasizes unities, anticipations, evolutions and layers of significance. His method, in contrast, emphasizes disunities or *differences*, a warning against all forms of anachronistic reading, antihermeneutical strategies which forego any hidden or subterranean meanings, and a horizontalized set of values focused upon practices and transsubjective structures.

The analyses based upon this method are, admittedly, often brilliant and clearly provide us with new perspectives upon historicocultural phenomena. Indeed, I would claim that Foucault provides us with the glimpse of a genuinely new way of doing intellectual history, but not without need of serious correction. The correction, I will contend, is one which must recapture within proper limits, precisely what Foucault throws out (continuities, similarities, levels, and, above all, a certain kind of context).

Indeed, even preliminarily, a contextual interpretation of Foucault, blended with a little standard philosophical self-reflexivity, might well yield a preliminary historical observation. Does Foucault not himself reflect a very current historical situation which he, in turn, tends to read anachronistically back into our history?

Let us take one strand of history developed in *The Order of Things*. What becomes biology for the contemporary era, has as its history a discontinuous set of refractions with respect to the plant and animal world. In the Medieval Period, plants and animals are described in terms of a multilayered set of meanings which include their physical characteristics, their symbolic significances, what is said about them in a historical, legendary favored authority context, etc. Their significance is ordered by a set of homologies and analogies. Then, for reasons which are never explained by Foucault, a gestalt switch occurs and when we come to the early Modern Period (his Classical Era), we find that the plant and animal world is now described in a radically different way. They are classified in a matrix which is based on what we might describe as "Cartesian" in that the multiple layers of meanings have been stripped down to a certain kind of geometric description. Plants belong to families by virtue of geometric shapes and numbers (numbers and shapes of petals, for example), and like the geometrical world which emerges later, are even described as if they existed only in black and white. Still later, and again after a gestalt switch, biology appears on the scene and now the "perceptual" characteristics of plants take back seat with respect to internal organic functions which presumably are below the level of perception. Anatomy and function become the focused values for a biological description.

I shall return to this refractive progression later with respect to perception—but for the moment take note of Foucault's own description. It is as if for some moment in intellectual history, one sees things in a certain way. Then, again precisely because of the rejection of connections and continuities, a radical gestalt switch occurs and the previous way of seeing things—never refuted, but simply abandoned—is replaced by a new set of structures.

How are we to deal with this progression of refractions? Permit me to suggest a very simple observation based upon a very old philosophical practice. What happens if we turn Foucault upon himself in a self-referential move? And this is a historically contexted way? First, an observation upon the very contemporary intellectual scene within which Foucault operates.

Those familiar with the contemporary French intellectual scene, particularly if they have the advantage of some distance, will recognize very rapidly its Parisocentric and faddish nature. A characterization might be as follows: Any strain of thought which gains enough momentum to be more than idosyncratic, and which with enough time to develop describable family characteristics, will be declared a movement and will probably involve the entire intellectual set of readers. (I only too well remember how impressed I was in 1967–68, my first year in Paris, when I found virtually everyone from students to architects to faculty, who were reading the new figures of the time. This was, after all, the very year in which Derrida published his first influential books.) But, equally, no sooner than is such an accomplishment absorbed and known, than the seeds of its demise are laid.

Once movements are recognized, explored for a time, but then characterized with specific features, then they are pronounced "dead." Thus we have seen the progression from the widely popular existentialism of the fifties be transformed into the phenomenology of the sixties, the structuralism of the seventies, and the post-structuralism of the eighties. (Foucault, perhaps recognizing this effanescence, early protested his affiliation with "structuralism" just as Sartre two decades earlier had protested his "existentialism." The structure of Parisocentric intellectual life is thus amazingly like the world of fashion described by Barthes.)

Thus in a cycle of eternal return, each new movement undergoes an often premature gestalt switch into something else and an intellectual death occurs, not by refutation or even necessarily telling critique, but by abandonment. When such a death occurs, moreover, there is no period of mourning. Instead there is an immediate battle by the surviving relatives for their share of the estate and a new cycle sets in.

On the North American scene, news of such distant deaths arrives more slowly and the inheritance fights are at best echoed differently. But the effect is felt. Phenomenology, which here matured more slowly than in Europe, has only recently come into its own. Yet recent relatives of post-structuralism have also arrived and are contesting the territory of Continental philosophy in certain ways. I have characterized this progression as a family fight and in part it is. But I hope to indicate that the very concept of gestalt switch, whether in perception or in history, owes its deeper understanding to ancestral phenomenology.

With respect to Foucault, we can now turn the observation into a self-referential one. Does Foucault reflect his own situation and time and anachronistically read it into the past? Stylistically, that is certainly a valid parallelism. One can almost read the interpretation of how plants and animals were described and the development of the refracted beginnings of a discipline as the anachronistic Parisocentrism of the present into the past.

There is one more observation I should like to make concerning Foucault before returning to the topic of perception. Obviously, there is an unspoken and implicit unity which must be presumed in Foucault's histories. However described, the *referent* to which description applies, across the switches from homology and analogy, to natural histories, to biology, is what may be called the plant and animal world. Foucault is certainly correct in pointing out how our understandings of these kingdoms have changed, particularly with respect to our cultural history. (And this, after all, is where post-structuralism focuses and excells. But with a price: only by bracketing the *referent world* can one focus upon the changing interpretative structures and bring them into focus. The result, is to draw back from the referent world and one has but to ask the question: would there likely ever be a post-structuralist natural science? Or is post-structuralism more likely to devolve only as interpretive cultural science?)

Similarly, there could be—and that is my take-off point—a similar reinterpretation of the history of perception within these refractions. But to show this, one must have a sufficiently deep and comprehensive theory of perception such that both its micro and macro characteristics are accounted for. And it is precisely here, I believe, that Merleau-Ponty may return to the scene.

Merleau-Ponty's Phenomenology and Perception

I have already alluded to two important features of a phenomenology of perception, both of which are evident in Merleau-Ponty. There is the multidimensionality of perception which occurred earlier in Husserl's phenomenology. Material things are transcendent, with depth and thickness. Having taken a brief excursion through Foucault, we can put this restoration to things in historical perspective. What the Modern or Classical era in Foucault's terms did, was to reduce the thing to a set of geometrical characteristics and to remove it from its historical context. This was simultaneously a reduction *to* "perception" and a reduction *of* perception. To perceive the plant kingdom as if it were a set of qualia, determined by shape and number, is not false, but is clearly inadequate. It reduces the richness of perception to one of its dimensions.

In this respect, Husserl clearly enacts a switch from the geometric reductionism of the Modern era. He restores the multidimensionality of perception. But in another respect, he too, remains restricted in his analysis. He does not replace the cultural for perception. And again by reading perception off a Foucaultean strategy, we may account for another aspect of the history of perception. Not only was perception reduced to its geometrical qualities in the Modern era, but it became identified solely and simply with what I call *microperception*. Microperception is strictly "sense" perception which in the Modern era, was thought to be the result of causal influences from a subperceptual world. The Husserlian restoration, then, was only partial. Perception for Husserl remained predominantly sense or microperception to which would have to be added by *apperception* other features.

Contrarily, insofar as perception is at least dealt with implicitly by Heidegger, what emerges is a strong sense of what I shall call the *macroperceptual*. There are two ways in which this dimension to perception may be symptomatically located. First, our interpretative understanding is clearly culturally-historically sedimented. This is the point of the whole deconstruction of metaphysics and the recognition that we can easily confuse what we actually experience in our pragmatic relation to equipment with a reduced cartesian interpretation of the same. But, secondly and much more profoundly, by including State-of-Mind (an emotional component, if you will) in the existentalia, Heidegger shows that all moods primitively reveal a World. This is to say that if interpreted as a kind of implicit perception, Heidegger breaks through the perception/ apperception distinction found in Husserl. This amounts to reading perception macroperceptually in my terms.

Merleau-Ponty capitalizes upon both these discoveries and in his theory of perception unites micro and macro levels. Perception thus becomes not only multidimensioned, but *multistable* or *polymorphic*. Perception in Merleau-Ponty is simultaneously sensory *and cultural*. We perceive culture and, conversely, at even the most micro-perceptual level we find polymorphy. So, if once again we read this trajectory of a phenomenology of perception via Foucault, we can directly appropriate Merleau-Ponty's suggestions about perception in aesthetics.

Renaissance perspective and Euclidianization of perception is both an historical and a perceptual event. The structural polymorphy of perception allows this to be the case. Similarly, the world which is revealed in all art may be the event for different world gestalts. This is to say that as a trajectory, we can begin to see the role of perception in its Merleau-Pontean sense, take different shapes in the refractions of history—the history which Foucault described for example. But to say this is to say no more than that in spite of Foucault, one can find a homology between at least existential phenomenology and Foucault's historical refractionism. More is needed. What is needed is to attain a depth structure which both accounts for the refractions and yet allows a more unitary central role for perception. In keeping with what seems to be emerging in what may be called "The Stony Brook School,"[4] I shall try to show that both these goals are attained in *hermeneutic perception*.

Hermeneutic Perception

Hermeneutic perception is derived from a Merleau-Pontean model. It is a synthesis of perception as both multidimensional and multistable, and it unites on a scale micro and macro dimensions of perception. Finally, it finds its interpretative clue in what I shall now call a refraction of contexts. But tactically, it also echoes an often forgotten Husserlian strategy—variational method.

I shall first demonstrate by way of concrete illustration, the major features of hermeneutic perception (you will recognize many of the key concepts derive from Merleau-Ponty):

Were I to ask the naive observer what is pictured above, the answer might be "It is a bird in flight." That, at least, is a statistically likely answer in that there is virtually a conventional sedimentation about such a configuration. Now, in terms of structural features of perception, the above drawing also illustrates what was for Merleau-Ponty a primitive of perception: a figure against a ground. The figure is focally selected out of a background.

Already, at this possibly simplest level, however, we can begin to locate the multidimensionality and the multistability or polymorphy of perception. The figure is always *seen as* both a sensory object *and* as a possible meaning. I would point out that to say it *is* a black, double curved line on a white background is already to have *seen as*. It is merely to have seen as in a more "geometric" interpretation than as the more common "bird figure" interpretation. Not to interpret—nonhermeneutic perception—is always to reduce either below or beyond the level of perception itself.

Let us also note, preliminarily, that in this simplest of figure/ground situations, the field or ground is empty and thus *open* to an easier polymorphy. This can be captured very easily by going through a series of perceptually imaginative variations or alternate hermeneutic contexts. The figure *could* be (a) for the high technology adolescent, not a bird, but the oncoming hang glider which he or she desires; (b) for the neo-Freudian, a set of upward pointing buttocks or breasts; or (c) for the geologist, two distant monadnocks (rounded hills); and so forth as the *ad infinitum* of our perceptual imagination can take us. Such is the polymorphy or ambiguity of essential perception.

This series of possibilities—the subject matter of all phenomenologically rigorous analyses—serves as a paradigm for all subsequent phenomenological ontology. Thus, if we were to project the paradigm into a Foucaultean intellectual history, we would note that any subject matter such as the plant and animal kingdom, offers just such a nonrigid set of possibilities which makes possible the refractions of Foucault's histories.

But so far, we have merely begun. The figure against an open or blank ground easily allows for the polymorphy. I wish now to show that polymorphy itself is not simply open indefinitely, but is graded with respect to the complexity and configuration of its arrangements. If we change the figure by filling in more of the ground, here as in a child's drawing, it becomes less likely that some of our previously equally likely variations remain plausible. The double curved lines could be birds, or even a little bit oddly, hang gliders, but now in the changed scene they are far less plausibly flying buttocks or elevated monadnocks. The situation is different and more determined. Here, of course, is a beginning clue to the role of embodiment in the Merleau-Pontean corpus. For example, the body plays an essential role in perception and the body is a concrete location from which perspectives are had—even if traditionally overlooked.

This is not to reduce polymorphy to nothing, however, but it is to contextually locate certain rather than other essential possibilities. It is, in my terms, to begin to come to grips with a *reference realm*. I may illustrate this both positively and negatively. Negatively, an embodied being is never and can never be the simultaneous observer of all that is except from a presumed panoramic point-of-view because to observe is to observe from a point of view. The world as seen by the philosopher's god is not possible for human embodied observers—but even more, the human descriptions of the view from the god's eye perspective always turns out to be one of panoramic or distant viewing. Even the descriptions subtly include latent phenomenologies of position. Thus "from above," "all encompassing," and other such terms applied visualistically, silently presuppose a distant panorama and the hidden embodiment of a possible position. There is no god's eye view, or if there is, it has never been described adequately by philosophers.

To have indirectly located this nexus of embodiment, however, in no way diminishes polymorphy. Let us here return to the Merleau-Pontean observation that perspective (in the Renaissance sense) is learned and thus historically located. What follows is a series of drawings or cultural representations from which we take note of certain perspectival features. I

begin with what is familiar to us in our now conventional sedimentations—elevated perspective.

If our problem is to represent, say, a garden and particularly its layout, two perspective views may be suggested. The one is an overhead view, displaying the garden as if seen directly from above—in today's world as if in an airplane over the landscape. This is the usual *map-perspective*. Note in passing that most of us are capable of picturing scenes in precisely this way in spite of the fact that we rarely so experience gardens in this way. An equally likely representation would be a partially elevated perspective (with or without the converging parallel lines of the Renaissance), as if one were on a tower in the foreground, looking down at the garden.

Such portrayals are interestingly cross-cultural, at least with respect to all "high civilizations." The example I have used is European, but similar drawings may be found in Indian, Japanese or Middle Eastern literature.

Such elevated points of view are perspectival—again with or without the geometrical rules of the Renaissance—and appear to occur cross-culturally in all complex interconnected civilizations. But they are also historical.

The position which we normally *do* actually have with respect to gardens is not elevated any higher than the position of our head against the ground (this is already elevated in degree by our upright posture), thus a more "natural" representation might well be one of a side-view of the garden. And that is exactly what we find in many more ancient portrayals, for example, this part of an Egyptian bas-relief:

But even at this early stage, a beginning approximation of elevated perspective appears to have been attempted, attempted in a way which probably appears "inconsistent" to us. For in this representation there is a mixed side view and overhead view (the vines and pillars of the water pond). The inconsistency, phenomenologically, comes from the necessity of the implicit viewer to occupy two different positions simultaneously. Perhaps here, too, is an early anticipation of Cubism with its fractured visual planes. What is more likely is that this representation is in fact familiar to a people whose writing is equally "inconsistent" from our point of view. Hieroglyphics is, after all, a composite of phonetic and pictographic writing. My own suspicion is that the bird's-eye view is deeply connected with the phenomenon of reading. The reader is positioned "above" the text and the text becomes the immediate field which is perceived, a mini "world" as it were.

Take now an example from a nonliterate people, in this case a bark painting by a tribe in Colombia, S.A:

Here is a "primitive" representation which merely scatters in space the figures, each of which presuppose their own individual *side view* perspective. Note that while the whole appears to be "from above," it is not so constructed. Rather each individual represented figure is seen from the side as in the Egyptian relief. But there is a fracturing of perspectival positions.

As Merleau-Ponty so deeply recognized, art illustrates perceptual possibilities and, in its depth, the polymorphy of perception. Or, is it from art that he discovered the polymorphy of perception? In either case both the multidimensionality and the multistability of perception is here demonstrated.

It is from the polymorphy, however, that the post-structuralists take their primary clues. A refractive paradigm recognizes that each possibility may be situated in a new gestalt, such that it may be made coherent—at least for a time or until challenged or abandoned by the intrusion of another refraction. And although it might well be possible to continue our analysis of pictures to show how each contains within itself a "world" perspective, a better illustration may be had from archeoastronomy.

A.T. Aveni has pointed out that ancient tropical astronomies are distinctly different from ancient temperate region astronomies.[5] Part of the reason is to be found in the essentially different celestial phenomena which may be seen from these two different parts of the earth. In the Northern Hemisphere—where most of the inhabited land mass is—there is one star which remains stationary overhead (the North Star or Polaris). Others trace a circular path overhead around Polaris; and still others rise and set in some angled path across the skies as do the sun and moon.

Contrarily, in the southern tropics and Oceania, there is no North Star, nor circular motion, but due to the position on the revolving planet, Earth, the position occupied by the ancient observer is one which sees stars rise and set almost vertically. Thus almost all these peoples developed some version of what we call a *sidereal compass*. That is, a "compass" which relates to the rising and setting of these stars and planets. *Some* temperate region astronomy also uses such a compass as well, since there are sufficient numbers of heavenly bodies which rise and set over the horizon—Stonehenge is the best known such compass in Europe.

We need to note what is involved here. If we use our habitual elevated perspective, the sidereal compass appears as a circle of markers from which measurements may be taken. The actual measurements are made from the middle or some fixed spot and the compass works only in relation to the actually fixed perceptual places foredetermined for the measurements.

Note that the actual user probably neither designs the compass from an elevated perspective, nor does it get used in that way. The actual use is dependent upon the fixed position for embodied perception. Thus what the observer sees is like this:

Now there is something quite interesting which appears to be virtually cross-cultural in much tropical archeoastronomy. The compass, taken as a symbol for the cosmos, is construed to be *square* and the corners and sides, associated with major celestial bodies' paths, are interpreted as pillars.

To us this may seem anomalous or at least odd, and if taken as a representation of the cosmos, false. But this is in part perceptually because our privileged perspective is habitually one "from above," from an elevated perspective. Thus how could the earth be a house and even square? But if our actual and our habitual privileged point of view were not elevated, but were on ground level, so to speak, then what are the perceptual effects? What the ancient astronomer or navigator actually sees (and assuming that the embodied position is also the privileged point of interpretation), then the "pillars" of the heavens are equivalently round or square. (And I have to add only one caveat to demonstrate the plausibility of this interpretation. If the paths are horizontally distant, as they are, then one cannot indeed tell which are closer or more distant due to the phenomenon of foreshortening. (We still cannot *perceive* which stars are closer and which farther in correspondence to anything told us by contemporary astronomers.)

This, then, is what is seen, and its hermeneutic context can just as equivalently be that of square (familiar as the house and thus culturally important center of life) or a circle (which might well occur in exactly the same way among peoples who build circular dwellings.)

Again, to return to Merleau-Ponty, I think I have at least illustrated, but perhaps more deeply confirmed that *culture is perceived*. Its polymorphy is embedded in the forms of life which we actually and imaginatively enact. But perception is *both* refractive *and* structural. It should be clear from my examples that there is the possibility of a great deal of variety and diversity—indeed, dizzyingly so—but that all such variety and diversity is also traceable to certain possibilities of perception as well. Even the most radically fractured perception, as in my bark painting or cubism, hides within itself the simplicities of embodiment, point of view and its possible multiplications. But the multidimensionality and the multistability of perception is so complex that we are far from exhausting its pathways.

And to illustrate this, I leave you with one more reversal, a piece of phenomenological or even post–Merleau-Pontean magic. I return to my ambiguous bird drawing.

In the Merleau-Pontean context, the simplest perception is a figure/ground gestalt, even if ambiguous. But figures and grounds are reversible. And as in Zen aesthetics, it well may be that the background is the subject which the foreground figure sets off. But there is another reversibility which may be suggested by this Eastern reversal. What if our "bird" is a cut in the foreground paper and is thus a "figure" against a hidden background?

Such deep reversals are probably rare, but they are suggestive of the need for a most critical and radical type of phenomenological analysis. To get beyond both Merleau-Ponty and the post-structuralist critics, what is needed is a demonstration of both the rich polymorphy of perception *and* its complexure of invariant structures. That is the task of the new phenomenology, the phenomenology which can both appreciate refractive polymorphism, but also situate it within the multidimensional act which is perception.

Chapter 3

Phenomenology, 'Metaphor-Metaphysics' and the Text

Continental philosophers, particularly those owing debts to the phenomenological-hermeneutic traditions, seem obsessed today with the written embodiment of Language: Ricoeur with narrative, Derrida with writing, and now, Gadamer on text. And, as professor Gadamer has pointed out, what we in America call the linguistic turn is also in its own way a preoccupation for Continental philosophers. But the two traditions have different paradigms and problems concerning language and interpretation.

Charles Taylor, in a seminal article, "Theories of Meaning," characterized these two traditions as *designative* and *expressive* theories of meaning. Within this difference there is also embedded a difference in the conception of what counts as foundational for Language. The Anglo-American tradition, dominantly designative, founds its architectonic upon the declarative, predicating statement, thus making problems of reference and the isolation of logical form the primary interests of philosophy. This places metaphor and other similar "complex" linguistic phenomena in a derivative position. I shall call such a theory explicitly *metaphysical* in the sense that its ideal is (a) foundational, (b) its paradigm meaning univocal or monodimensioned, and (c) its tactic reductive in that philosophical work consists of either reducing complex expressions to logically simple ones, or in isolating in a translation of ordinary expressions, the presumed logical structure of statements.

Contrarily, Continental or expressive theories of Language take their paradigm and foundation from what is today called *metaphor*. And whatever else metaphor may be, it is at least an expression which is multidimensional in meaning. Thus, inverse to designative theories, expressive theories see designative statements as derivative from the primal metaphor and as reductions to what is frequently called "dead metaphors." This family of theories owes a debt to Romanticism as Gadamer pointed out, and a good case of such a theory may be found in Heidegger's *Being and Time* where apophantic logic is seen as a derivative from primordial *Rede* or Discourse. Such a tradition, I shall hope to suggest, remains *implicitly* metaphysical in that the very notion of metaphor is inextricably tied to a metaphysics. I shall return to this point later.

We then have theories which are in one sense the converse and obverse of each other, with Anglo-American designative theories building upon logical primitives or simples up to complex, "ambiguous" phenomena such as metaphor, and expressive theories which found Language in the complex primitive from which by reduction logical simples are derived.

If Quine is right in what I call his phenomenology of theories—that theories are onion shaped and peel selectively— and I think he is right, then we might expect to find selective biases in what the two families take as their "texts." And that is frequently the case. The analytic philosophies have been most comfortable with technical texts such as those found in the sciences, and relatively more perplexed with such texts as those of theology (which is already a good step or two removed from sacred texts from which theology itself is derived). Thus in the early days of analytic philosophical theology, the MacIntyre, Hare and Flew group consistently sought to find some nugget of literal truth claim, but found this a messy and difficult business, often ending in concepts like "bliks" or predispositions of subjects not subject to verification or falsification. The aim remained one of unpeeling theological language down to some presumed typical assertion of predicative statement. A more recent strategy is to take some phenomenon not itself linguistic—the plastic arts for example- and first "translate" this phenomenon into a cryptolanguage. This is the strategy of Nelson Goodman's *Languages of Art*. What we see here is a kind of rapproachement with the spirit of

Continental currency in that languages of art are clearly metaphorical in some sense. (This is certainly not to claim Goodman for Continental philosophy!) But it is to suggest that what he does—to my way of thinking quite artificial with respect to the phenomena—does parallel what I also perceive to be a current danger in the contemporary preoccupation with the embodiment of Language in its written form. That is to extend this preoccupation metaphorically to a model for Reality itself, or at least to allow written language to stand for Language.

In order not to be led too quickly into that temptation here, I propose to undertake the positive part of my approach by a deliberate return to an "old fashioned" phenomenological tactic, the turn to *perception* and perceptual objects. I shall use this turn as a different kind of paradigm for what follows.

I shall not here trace, in the usual laborious phenomenological fashion, either the method or its steps, but shall look directly at phenomenological results: what are the dimensions of the perceptual object, phenomenologically analyzed?

—First, all perceptual objects are *located in* and *relative to* a perceptual field and are never simples in themselves. To anticipate the parallelism with texts, we may say they are *contexted*. To forget or overlook this is to make the same elementary mistake as logical atomism and implicitly assume that there is one and only one meaning to a given object.

—Because perceptual objects are contexted, and because these contexts change with it the object-role, we may see that all perceptual objects are *multistable*. They may assume variations within variant contexts, but are invariantly located in some ratio with the field or context.

—And, all perceptual objects are multidimensional—this in a number of ways, but for purposes here I shall concentrate upon one of these. Husserl's analysis of the perceptual object differed from, say, classical empiricist analyses in pointing out that the object shows itself as copresently a manifest profile and a latent "meant" aspect in a ratio of present and absent. Thus in contrast to classical empiricist analyses which take note only of present "surfaces," the phenomenological analysis takes account of the transcendancy of the object in its latently given, but "absent" dimension.

These features do not exhaust the classical phenomenological analysis of the perceptual object, but they will do for purposes here. I shall now briefly illustrate each of these points in concrete examples.

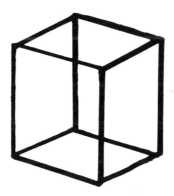

First, imagine an actual three-dimensional cube con-structed from white plastic, and note what happens when we see it in an actual situation.[1] In looking at it, we focus upon it, while pushing to the background its taken-for-granted context, i.e., its location in the actual visual surroundings. Yet while these surroundings are background, the object takes its place within and relative to that context.

Second, this object is multistable in the sense that were the context to change—for example if the cube were a part of a contemporary sculpture as a piece of the whole—it would also change in a perceptual sense.

Third, its multidimensionality is what it is precisely in the ratio and play of present and absent previously suggested. Were I to turn the cube around, you as viewer would get successively different profiles or *Abschatuungen* as Husserl called them—first one face, then another would appear, but with each change what was previously seen takes its place as the "meant" copresent backside with its invariant perceptual significance of having-a-backside. And while this significance is phenomenologically present and belongs equiprimordially to the object, it is such that it is present as to-be-given. (Were one of the faces, when I turn the object, to be colored differently, you might have been slightly surprised in that the meant significance is open to this possibility even though not necessarily anticipated, but were the object to simply disappear when turned, surprise would be astonishment.) All of this is ordinary fare for those familiar with phenomenological analyses, but now I shall introduce the twist needed to make the points which apply to metaphor-metaphysics.

Our cube, previously selected, experienced and focused upon, may begin to play a *metaphoric role*. It takes a special place within our experience and we carry that selection and focus over to a second set of related possible experiences. In a second example we may switch our attention from the three-dimensional cube to a two-dimensional drawing. And in our familiarity, we immediately recognize the drawing as a drawing *of* a cube:

The immediate assumption carried in our previously focused attention to the cube, is that the drawing is *of* a cube. Indeed, it is the famous Necker cube of perceptual psychology. And, truly, the drawing may appear *as* a cube—that is one of its perceptual possibilities or profiles. Moreover, since we are all sedimented in this mini-tradition of metaphor-metaphysics, we are probably also anticipating the common psychologists insight that the cube has not one, but two possible profiles. (It may be seen with this side facing forward, or be reversed with that side forward—as if the cube tilts differently.)

But why should we be led to see this drawing as a cube at all? I am suggesting that our metaphor-metaphysics pre-disposes us in that direction. In so doing, however, it covers over the other possibilities of the drawing.[2] Why should not the drawing be simply a two-dimensional object? Such a possibility could appear if it were contexted differently.

Imagine, now, that instead of a drawing, I were to present you with a wire frame (the outside hexagonal lines), connected to an inner frame (the central parallelogram shape), by six rubber bands. This wire and rubber construction is colored black and appears against a white ground.[3] Now were I to twist the construction around as with the actual three-dimensional cube, you would immediately see that the construction is "flat." Indeed, were it to be seen end on, it would appear as a black "line." And then by returning to its appearance against the white ground, we could see that it is a two-dimensional figure. (While we could now see its two-dimensionality, it remains possible even though understanding the construction for what it is, to recapture the three-dimensionality of the cube-drawing as well, but these are now simply other possibilities of the configuration.)

Nor do these three possibilities (forward facing and rearward facing cube and two-dimensional figure) exhaust the possibilities. Might I not take the inner parallelogram shaped frame and stretch it either towards you or away from you, revealing that to other three-dimensional effects incongruent with the cube-appearances, are also possibilities of the drawing? (We now have five perceptual possibilities or profiles and have begun to break the hold of the implicit sedimentation of what I am calling metaphor-metaphysics.)

Now I have simultaneously illustrated two things: first, the essential multistability of the perceptual object, and two, the way in which sedimented habits—which can be metaphor-metaphysics—may incline us to see only some possibilities. And, thirdly, I am implicitly claiming that only a *radical, phenomenological theory of variations* can open up this sedimentation. This is a short lesson in "phenomenological seeing."

But does the same apply to Language? And to the text? I think it does. If we make a quick isomorphic transfer of the lesson to Language, we might make the following observations:

—Language is contextual—*and I would claim differently contextual in spoken, compared to written embodiments.*[4] What is said is said against a background, in ordinary conversation against the here and now background of the situation. What is written, against its original field, and then repeated in the context of being read in a different time and place.

—Language is multistable. Its polymorphy is such that a single word or phrase means differently in different contexts. Derrida's play on heliotrope (as flower, then as dashed word "helio-trope" as a word-play) does not introduce it as a color. Or, the phrase, "to knock you up" in the context of England merely means to call upon one, but in the American context carries a different meaning. Multistability is closely linked to the ratio between expressions and their contexts and the ratio is different in spoken as compared to written contexts.

—Language is multidimensional. What is said has both a present, perhaps obvious meaning, but presents itself equiprimordially as an absent "backside" of the unsaid, pregnant with a multiple set of possibilities belonging essentially to the said. In logic, what is said assumes a large, silent background—a virtual metaphysics—to be understood at all. That is why logic must be *taught*, and particularly if it is symbolic logic. And Freud has made us aware of the silent meanings of jokes and slips of the tongue, which "say" more than we "intend."

In this suggestive isomorphism between perception and language, the Continental theories of language find their justification for the primacy of metaphor. For metaphor is the paradigm of a contextual, multistable and multidimensional expression. It is also an implicit place from which to critique a certain kind of metaphysics.

That kind of metaphysics of Language is, as mentioned, one which seeks to *reduce* expression to univocal meaning; to translate ambiguous or multistable expressions to linear ones; and to juridically reconstruct language according to the demands of logical form. That is why Rorty's observation that analytic philosophers should better be thought of as "lawyers of language" than as scientists is appropriate. (That is also why the result of analytically written work is far from genuine ordinary language, but reconstructed in a philosophical legalese understood only by professionals.)

But, just as the Anglo-American theories display a selective bias in what is chosen for analysis, so also does the Continental selectivity display itself in its choices. The *literary* text, or, as Gadamer points out in the close historical association between hermeneutics and theology, the exegetical exercise with "sacred" texts are the more frequently chosen examples. These are examples which display immediately the multidimensionality and multistability of the metaphorical. Thus as with analytic philosophy, so with the Continental selectivities there is a kind of self-verifying circle at work.

That in itself is not harmful, particularly since one could

argue that the more complex phenomenon of the sacred or literary text is at least richer and potentially more interesting to analyse. But there is today a second move which is made which escalates the stakes in this hermeneutical game. It is the move which makes "text" itself metaphorical. "Text" is taken as the paradigm of Reality or at least of Language and reverts to a different metaphysics, a metaphor-metaphysics.

Metaphor-metaphysics functions as the cube did for the drawing, to predipose us to a certain view, to consolidate it from a privileged example. To choose texts or particularly a kind of text—juridical for example—is to choose a pre-disposition.

Such a move is exemplified most enigmatically in Derrida. When he inverts the usual phenomenological preference for the primacy of *speech* into the primacy of writing, of inscription, of text, he performs a metaphysical move. And all of his qualifications do not obliterate that move since writing is claimed to "precede" speech (and in so doing becomes even more clearly metaphorical). The very critique of the "logo-centric," the "photological," the "metaphysics of presence" becomes first an inversion of the traditional selectivities, but simultaneously he falls prey to the same possibility of countercritique.

Gadamer is more subtle, yet one could suspect that his preference for the model of translation from a foreign tongue or in his selection of juridical examples that a similar temptation is to be found. Phenomenology, taken in its most radical sense, should be the forewarning that any selectivity, though necessary to say anything, must itself be critically scrutinized.

Phenomenology, at least in its original sense, is radically antimetaphysical. That is so with respect to the type of metaphysics I have characterized as the foundational, univocal or monodimensioned and reductive interpretation of pheno-mena. At least this is the potential trajectory of pheno-menology. To see this, one must revert to a central but often overlooked aspect of phenomenological interpretation. Too often the "negative theology" of the reductions has been focused upon, and too infrequently has the positive insight supplied by phenomenology been utilized. That insight is the use of variational method to understand invariants or structural relationships. To do a radical phenomenological interpretation, one must mightily resist both too quick closure and too easy foundational conclusions. And while in the limits of this context I cannot perform such a set of variations, I can suggest both historically and potentially what such a task would involve for hermeneutics.

Language, I contend, is invariantly always *embodied*. Even in logic, I would hold, one cannot find "propositions" apart from actual language. Language, like the subject, is always incarnate materially. Phenomenologists like Merleau-Ponty have recognized this. But while Language is always embodied, its embodiments are *variant*. This, too, is implicitly recognized and has been dealt with in the recent traditions of phenomenological philosophy. Indeed, the very debate today between hermeneutic and deconstructionist tendencies is illustrative of this fundamental variation.

One can juxtapose, for example, Merleau-Ponty and Derrida. The one argues for the primacy of *speech* incarnate in spoken sound: the other for the primacy of *writing*. But taken in the more radical sense this turns out not to be a debate, but a set of exercises on the phenomenologies of the verbal embodiment of Language varied with the inscriptional embodiment of Language. Only when the recalcitrant and vestigial metaphysical interpretation tempts one to premature foundational closure does the "debate" emerge. What is needed is to see that speech and writing are variant embodiments of Language—and in a sense this is partly pointed to by Gadamer. Prior to the too swift closures, we need a thorough and more radical set of regional phenomenologies of speech and writing.

But even this set of different variations is not yet sufficient. Again, within the limits of a radical phenomenology, adequacy cannot be claimed without exploring the essential field of possibilities. Only then can essential insight be claimed over empirical or historical actualities. I wish to suggest, precisely along the lines opened by my previous multistable illustrations, that we have not yet exhausted the variations upon the embodiments of Language.

I will not make a McLuhanesque point here, but a phenomenological one. *Language today is beginning to be embodied in a different way.* One of the contrasts between verbal embodiment of Language in speech and written embodiment in a text, has been with respect to history and time. Verbal speech once was restricted to the here-and-now of a present context; written speech was at least usually restricted to having-been-written and thus to some sense of past time (even if a little while ago and unless the reader was reading simultaneously with the writer). These make for variant meaning-context situations.

Today, on cinema and television and the taping of both audiovisual and of verbal speech, a new variation is had which displays both a past context like writing, and a present sense of living presentation in word and gesture. In a related way, the "languages" of artificial languages and symbolic languages embody Language in yet a different way, a soundless and wordless way. All of these are variants upon our previously familiar embodiments of Language.

I am suggesting that both deconstruction and her-meneutics, in their present preoccupation with the written embodiment of Language, with the text, may be ironically "out-of-date" in one sense. Derrida may be guilty of the same type of error he accused Husserl of in *Speech and Phenomena*, i.e., to have made speech foundational is to have prematurely closed, when the variant of writing must also be consider. Similarly, though less blatantly, it may be that a premature closure is implied in Gadamer's claim that the hermeneutic problems for speech and writing are the same.

I am trying to suggest that we now have a new task facing us, at the least the task of a new regional ontology, the analysis of an emergent embodiment of Language, related to but different from both speech and writing. And presumably well done, such a variation can perhaps better inform us about the invariants within Language itself.

In his early, controversial work on computers and artificial intelligence, Hubert Dreyfus argued that computers need bodies in order to think. Put negatively in his article by that name, he concluded that computers, because they didn't have bodies, could not think. But his conclusion is partly wrong: computers *do* have bodies, although their "brain" is not of the "wetware" type ours is. They have different "bodies." (And thus their "thinking" is also different.)

And it is here that we return to the problem of metaphor. A metaphor establishes *both* a likeness and a difference. Our penchant, however, is consistently to dwell on the likeness.

This was the case in the earlier theologies dealing with the analogies concerning God. It took a David Hume to point out the logical equivalence of metaphorical analogies—God could be as much like a spider as like a human as like a machine. The same critique could be applied today to the penchant of those in artificial intelligence to look for analogies between the computer and the mind.

It may turn out, however, that the more interesting and the genuinely new will come more out of the *differences*. For example, already in various pattern recognition and diagnostic programs it is precisely the different "intentionality" or selectivity of the computer which reveals new insights into such phenomena as thyroid disease and demographic switches.

I am not trying here to be either an apologist for the electronic age, nor for high technology as such. What I am suggesting, while at first seemingly oblique to this discussion, is that embodied in this development is another set of possibilities not yet fully understood with respect to the possible embodiments of language. Beyond the phenomenology of speech, and the implicit phenomenology of writing heretofore partly undertaken, there needs to be yet a further study of variations within the field of Language.

Potentially such a suggestion continues, as in traditional phenomenology, to reject metaphysics as defined in this context, and to refuse to reify either "text" or "metaphor." The subterranean bond between metaphysics and metaphor continues to dominate even the Continental theories of Language, and needs to be transcended. I suggest the use of critically applied variational method is the therapy which makes the first step in this direction. It's to open a new and rigorous, but nonfoundational interpretation of Language.

I am suggesting that we take the difference seriously, and call for the phenomenological investigation of a new set of possibilities.

Part II
Technics

Chapter 4

Technology and the Human; From Progress to Ambiguity

An intellectual and thematic awareness of the impact of technology is a recent phenomenon. In philosophy the first work to specifically treat a "philosophy of technology" did not appear until 1877: Ernst Kapp, *Grundlinien einer Philosophie der Technik*. And in North America the presumably comprehensive *Encyclopedia of Philosophy* still contains no entries under philosophy of technology or technics. Similarly, religious and theological thought, until this century, has also left the materiality of technology in the background. And when, in midcentury, the religious thinker, Jacques Ellul, and the philosopher, Herbert Marcuse, began to thematize technology, it was as if technology had already become a total and an ultimate threat to human spirit, the theme common to *The Technological Society* and *One Dimensional Man*. It is as if the spiritual disciplines of religious thought and philosophy arrived too late upon the scene.

Yet what contemporary humans in the technologically developed countries experience is obviously and saturatedly textured by technology. There are virtually no human activities today which do not implicate technologies: sexuality (birth control techniques), health (the high technologies of modern medicine), shelter ("machines for living"), and even the simple daily processes of awakening and eating (alarm technologies and kitchen hardware) are so shaped. But what is more telling is the way in which the ultimate threats to human existence have shifted to technological implicative possibilities.

Nuclear weaponry poses the possibility of an end with a "bang" for the entire species and the industrially stimulated speed of a greenhouse effect threatens a possible end of much life with a "whimper." Both ends are exacerbated by the now *geological* force of human developed technologies.

Technics—the human use of artifacts to transform a lifeworld, employed through skills or techniques—are, however, as old as humankind itself. And the impact of technics even in that dim past is beginning to be recognized.

From the Ice Ages on, we have become aware of the technological force of humans upon both local and regional territories. Humans were the probable cause of the extinction of some large mammals through overkill. The systematic use of fire presumably changed vast woodlands to prairie environments. And in early historic times salt sedimentation from irrigation toxified entire Middle East regions and deforestation created an irreversible change of climate in the Mediterannean. And even now migratory peoples with simple technologies and the techniques of domestication of grazing animals, continue to be implicated in the desertification of areas in marginal rainfall regions. Only slightly more advanced technologies today are decimating the rain forests.

Today, we have become aware that technics, now deployed through science and embodied in industrial-corporate systems have raised that amplification of technology to the level of a global force. This recognition that human technics now amplify our best and worst tendencies to the geological level has also begun to make us have doubts about what was dominantly the naive progressivism of previous centuries, particularly the nineteenth.

The idea of progress has been the cultural motor which has driven much of technological civilization. Its roots, though originating in Christianity, took secular shape as early as Fontenelle who elaborated the first genuinely secular theory of progress in his *Digression on the Ancients and the Moderns* (1688). By the next century progress is proclaimed inevitable by Marquis de Condorcet in his *Sketch for a Historical Picture of the Progress of the Human Mind* (1794). The work was completed on the eve of his own execution by guillotine, the mechanized headsman of the French Revolution, itself the model of the modern secular revolution.

Despite the fact that early modern science was already a technological science—da Vinci's diaries indicate that he, not unlike the current academic establishment, spent large amounts of time seeking funding through engineering projects to support his speculations—technics as such was not seen as a primary force. It took the Industrial Revolution to introduce the beginning awareness of ambiguity. During the nineteenth century one can find, side by side, writers who extoll the beauty of industrially enhanced sunsets with others who began to worry about effects upon human labor and alienation. Taylorism and Marxism arise in the same climate.

By the twentieth century, however, strong dystopian views began to take a much more dominant role. So prevalent have dystopian views been that writers, such as Samuel Florman in *The Existential Pleasures of Engineering* (1975) can display an almost romantic nostalgia for the faith in the engineer and the era of naive acceptance of inevitable progress. Not that the proclamation of progress is absent from the contemporary era. With every breakthrough technology a new announcement of revolutionary change with implied progress is made. The most obvious such example today is in the computer domain with advertising campaigns directed at convincing people that without computer skills their children will not be able to competently enter the twenty-first century. The same pattern of breakthrough, predicted revolutionary consequences, implied solution to social problems, continues, but now on a more regional basis. Moreover, with every such announcement there arises the accompaniment of doubt as well. Automation produces fears of unemployment; information accumulation and retrieval conjures possible invasions of privacy; genetic engineering causes worries over eugenic experimentation. Nor can the intelligent individual miss the major anomalies associated with our technologies. Again the most dramatic anomaly is in the nuclear arena where, with every increase of weaponry in power and speed, we seem to have less power to diplomatically control the outcome. But a wider public is also aware that with every promised solution there seem to be unexpected and frequently highly negative "side effects." In agriculture, the once utopian claimed green revolution is now seen to systematically be tied to the massive use of chemical fertilizers and pesticides which, in turn, change environmental factors whose negative effects may include carcinogens or the extinction of species through the toxification of a food chain (DDT, EDB, PBCs, and the like). In medicine, many wonder drugs turn out also to be mutagenic or toxic (DES, for example). In short, the belief in an *unmitigated* good through technological progress has been shaken and replaced by a strong sense of ambiguity.

The anomalies of technological civilization point up the need for serious *interpretation*. The interpretive sciences, too, have been sedimented in a dominant view which implicitly and sometimes explicitly overlooks anomaly. The anomaly has its roots in the dominant paradigm of interpretation which has suppressed technics and its role. The standard view holds that, with the rise of modern science, a new and essentially different kind of technology emerged, scientific-technology. This technology, subsequently embodied in corporate and industrial organization, becomes the global force that we now recognize. The tendency to so interpret technics is common to both the traditions of reflective religious and philosophical disciplines. In the religious context, materiality is often seen as "symbolic" in function, secondary to, or at most the expression of an immaterial spirit. Philosophically, technology is "applied" theory dependent on "science" which arises from pure thought. Only when technologies become raised to global status are they recognized as having inintended "Frankenstein" properties which were unseen. These make it imperative that we deal with the results which now face humankind in spite of our failures to predict them.

What is needed, interpretatively, is a more adequate paradigm if the role of technics and the human is to be understood. The argument here will be that such a paradigm may be hinted at through a new set of interpretative tools. These concepts, which have arisen simultaneously and independently, are in effect a change in interpretative perspective. Its sources are multiple, but appearances of such a shift may be seen symptomatically in the initial work in the history and philosophy of science performed in the sixties by Thomas Kuhn on the North American scene and paralleled during the same period with respect to the origins of the social (human) sciences by Michel Foucault in Europe.

Both thinkers shifted what had been the dominance of an evolutionary, accumulative and virtually linear model of science-interpretation to a much more disjunctive, refractive model which emphasizes "revolutions" and "paradigm shifts." In the process new possibilities for interpretation which now may be applied to human technics also emerge. The success of the revolutionary or gestalt switch models with respect to the sciences is quite obvious today. Insights from this new model are now used by scientists themselves, as for example in D.L. Anderson, "The Earth as Planet: Paradigms and Paradoxes," (*Science*, 27 January 1984). (The article describes an inversion of many of the presumed causes of continental drift and plate techtonics through new insights provided by extraterrestrial observation.)

This shift of emphasis from a simple, linear perspective to a more refractive one is itself a change in intellectual history and may be applied to other aspects of historical interpretation, including technics. By making technics the fulcrum of vision, the variables which surround it also change. For example, if the actual *praxis* of what we take as prehistoric "religion" is taken as an example, we may begin to see how our own understanding of "magic" changes.

Technics *as* religion was what we once termed *magic*. Indeed, most magic utilizes tools in ritual praxis in an attempt to modify events. The shaman who waves a feather fan over the ill person, or who extracts stones from the head of the patient, is using a technology in a religious context. The usual interpretation of this phenomenon, however, reveals more about the anachronistic way in which the contemporary can project his belief context upon a previous one than upon the practice itself. Thus to see the shamanistic praxis as a poor or inappropriate use of technique-technology, as if it were not yet "scientific" in the contemporary sense, is to miss the entire interpretative context which fits the occasion. This is not to deny that the trajectory of desire—to rid the patient of the evil-disease-pain—runs through the centuries and practices involved. Magic-religion-technics in this context is multi-dimensional and plays social as well as physical roles.

In our own history the connection of technics with actual religious praxis is equally overlooked or deliberately sup-pressed. Prayers, meditative practices, rituals may, of course, not utilize tools or artifacts, and may be purely techniques—but this is rarely the case. The materiality and use of crucifixes, icons, chalices, in Christian praxis is usually taken to be either merely incidental or at most symbolic. But not unlike the shaman, the question arises as to what effect would emerge if all the artifacts were in fact removed? What remains common to the shamanistic context and the Western context is what may be called the *hermeneutic* dimension of technics. This is a technics which is utilized interpretatively, in an analogue with language rather than as an extension of bodily skills.

Thus while our view of religion may have been too disembodied, blind to the role of technics, similarly our view of technology may have been too narrowly understood as a "physical" force limited to an implicit model of the body and its extensions. Contemporary technics, as for example in computers, make the hermeneutic dimension of technology appear more starkly even if that dimension has always been present.

There are reasons why this set of implications gets underplayed. In the span of Western religious traditions, those which are anti-iconographic (some aspects of Judaism, most Protestantism, etc.) have often prevailed. Thus the most obviously "magical" interpretative relations based upon visual semblances (the icon of Mary "resembles" the Holy Mother) are rejected by these traditions even though what has actually occurred is the substitution of a different set of technics and a different hermeneutic context. The anti-iconographic traditions *have* utilized a vast set of technologies focused in written technologies (Bibles, texts, writing, etc.) which embody the various theologies of Word. Technics pervades both traditions, but in different ways and with different sets of hermeneutic uses.

A perspective which so focuses upon the materiality of technics in all human praxis, also points to certain newer aspects of our understanding of technology. One essential and invariant dimension of technology has always been its potential and actual amplificational power. Our tools and weapons have from the beginnings allowed the human species to prevail over other more naturally strong species and within our species for those with more amplificational power to prevail over those with less.

A similar overloking of the role of technics in science may be noted. Just as either the icon or the text "embodies" and transmits religion, so instrumentation "embodies" contemporary science. Indeed, without instrumentation contemporary science could not exist since its primary fields of inquiry at the micro and macro levels are made present only through the technologies of instrumentation. While such is now clearly an *essential* dimension to science, the view that technology is "applied" science still obtains. What is needed is a more radical paradigm shift if the role of technics in human activity is to be understood.

The first step in such an interpretation is one which both takes a very long range view of the variant ways in which science has been embedded culturally in our history, and which utilizes the clues which identify period of "normal" science. Both Foucault and Kuhn have independently noted that such clues are better found in repeaters of a tradition and its sediments, than in originators (as for example in text books, manuals, writings of apologists. etc.) Thus while it is commonplace to contrast classical Greek science as purely contemplative and speculative with modern science as experimental, what is missed is the way that science was culturally embedded in a way in which technics from the beginning was incorporated.

Greek science, far from being only a theoretical and speculative activity, contained quite explicitly existential functions. Thus even as late as its transmission into Roman culture—a culture better characterized by its engineering exploits than its science—one finds the "normal" paradigm of Greek thought echoed from Democritus, to Epicurus and continued by Lucretius in *De Rerum Natura*:

> I will set out to discourse to you on the ultimate realities of heaven and the gods. I will reveal those atoms from which nature creates all things and increases and feeds them and into which, when they perish, nature again resolves them . . .[1]

After setting forth this by then conventional atomism, Lucretius describes its existential purpose which sets it against the popular religions of the time as a kind of secular demythologization:

> When human life lay grovelling in all men's sight, crushed to
> the earth under the dead weight of superstition . . . a man of
> Greece was first to raise mortal eyes in defiance, first to
> stand erect and brave the challenge. Fables of the gods did
> not crush him . . . the vital vigour of his mind prevailed.[2]

This existential function, a kind of "power" of mind, however
shows no hint of using or overcoming nature. To the contrary,
this paradigm is contemplative and distancing. Its only hubris
is to know the whole:

> As soon as your reasoning, spring from that god-like mind,
> lifts up its voice to proclaim the nature of the universe, then
> the terrors of the mind take flight, the ramparts of the world
> roll apart, and I see the march of events throughout the
> whole of space.[3]

Here is a science which distances human woes from their
material base; which destroys superstitions; and which seeks to
know the whole. But its means and ends are speculative and
there is no hint of any connection to a technics.

A similar look, not at originators, but at those who have
already accepted a paradigm as normal, reveals that by the
sixteenth century a massive and taken-for-granted shift in the
way science was culturally embedded had taken place. Francis
Bacon's second and third aphorisms point up the change.

> The unassisted hand and the understanding left to itself
> possess little power. Effects are produced by the means of
> instruments and helps, which the understanding requires no
> less than the hand; and as instruments either promote or
> regulate the motion of the hand, so those that are applied to
> the mind prompt or protect the understanding.[4]

Here is a technologically embodied science which, even when
technics is metaphysically extended to conceptual tools, is
instrumentally extended. Moreover, the new formula that
knowledge-power, power to change or overcome nature and
not merely to contemplate it, is simultaneously announced.

> Knowledge and human power are synonymous, since the
> ignorance of the cause frustrates the effect; for nature is only
> subdued by submission, and that which in contemplative

philosophy corresponds with the cause in practical science becomes the rule.[5]

Moreover, this new paradigm is so deeply embedded by the sixteenth century that Bacon's contemporary, Christopher Marlowe, can play the dystopian to Bacon's new utopianism. Thus in "Dr. Faustus," the doctor sells his soul to the Devil to obtain precisely the arcane knowledge-power over nature which allows him to make changes at will. Faustus wants the science which the Evil Angel describes:

> Go forward, Faustus, in that famous art
> Wherein all nature's treasury is contained:
> Be thou on earth, as Jove is in the sky,
> Lord and commander of these elements.[6]

What emerged from the Renaissance was thus not only an experimental science, nor merely a new technique of measurement and use of mathematics, but a *technological* science simultaneously embodied in instrumentation and tied culturally to a sense of power techniques. Moreover, this power paradigm was implicit from its Renaissance beginnings. Machiavelli's treatises are modern power techniques, da Vinci's researches are strikingly modern in part because they are simultaneously engineering exercises embedded in the rise of the early "military-industrial complex." Power technics and science are interlocked at the beginnings of modern as contrasted with classical science.

It has been left to the work of Lynn White, Jr. to demonstrate that the missing connection between classical and modern science lies in the virtual technological revolution of the Medieval Period which both historically and conceptually preceded and underlay the Latin rise of modern science. Thus as early as the ninth centuries, the western European search for power began with the development and distribution of large machine technologies, most notably in wind and water mills. Machine power continued its development through the high Middle Ages in the construction of major public projects such as the cathedrals, cities, the spread of commerce, and later the voyages of discovery. Each of these activities employed large power machinery such as cranes, vessels, drills, all with circular motion and machine gearing such as would dominate nineteenth century industry. Nor should one ignore the extent to which such technologies as clocks changed the very perception of and representation of time. In short, prior to the rise of modern science as it emerged in its Baconian form, the "invention of invention" had already occurred; civilization had employed technology to enact its religious destiny to "subdue and multiply and have dominion over the earth." White concludes: "By the early fourteenth century, then, Europe showed not only an unmatched dynamism in technology; it also arrived at a technological attitude toward problem solving which was to become of inestimable importance for the human condition."[7]

To this point what is established is a sense of the paradigm shift which differentiates the contemplative, speculative science of classical thought from the technologically embodied and power focused technics of modern science. But while both versions are differently culturally embedded, the dominant understanding is one which retains the view that technology extends science, that science "applies" technology. Yet a deeper paradigm shift is possible, a shift which inverts this usual way of understanding the contemporary relationship between science and technology.

The twentieth century philosopher, Martin Heidegger, made precisely this suggestion. In his famous "Question Concerning Technology," (1953) he argues that technology is ontologically prior to science and that science, far from being the origin of technology, is its necessary tool. And although such an interpretation seems not only to run counter to the dominant view, but to be counter-intuitive, it does provide another perspective from which to understand technology and the human.

Heidegger's thesis is that technology is not simply a collection of tools neutrally used by humans—this would be a subjective-anthropological definition—but is a way of seeing. Through technology the world is revealed in a particular way, as what would now be called a "resource well" (*Bestand*). Nature, its objects and relations, are understood in a certain way. This perspective, a technological ontology, thus calls for a means of dealing with nature consonant with its interpretation and that means is science:

Modern science's way of representing pursues and entraps nature as a calculable coherence of forces. Modern physics is not experimental physics because it applies apparatus to the question of nature. The reverse is true. Because physics, indeed already as pure theory, sets nature up to exhibit itself as a coherence of forces calculable in advance, it orders its experiments precisely for the purpose of asking whether and how nature reports itself when set up this way.[8]

The aim or essence of technology is both cultural and ontological. It "sees," takes nature in a certain way, and "enframes" it. For this reason, Heidegger argues, technology is prior to science:

> Because the essence of modern technology lies in enframing, modern technology must employ exact physical science. Through its so doing the deceptive illusion arises that modern technology is applied science.[9]

In this inversion of the usual interpretation, the very purity of theory functions as the tool of, the application of the metaphysics of "resources." Thus both science and technology are embedded in a particular cultural trajectory. Neither are neutral and both are part of an earlier metaphysical position.

That position can now be seen to be consonant with the first major paradigm shift from its ancient roots. Baconian science, already embodied technologically, wedded to the West's long hunger for power evident in the technological revolution of the Middle Ages, reaches its result in a foundational view of nature as "resource well" there for human use. The historical echo reaches as far back as the Genesis injunction to "have dominion."

What the inversion of the interpretation of science and technology does, however, is to begin to make the anomalies of contemporary technics more understanding. First, by re-locating the role of science with respect to technology, the view that science is neutral, even as a tool, is demythologized. Nor is it possible that a purely theoretical science unleashes simply unintended consequences which produce a Franken-steinian effect at the technological level. Rather, the "danger" which lies within the essence of modern technology, according to Heidegger, is there from the beginning in the very way in which the world is revealed. For whatever the understanding of nature as reality there may be, it ultimately encompasses the human as well. And this is the case with nature as resource well (Bestand). If nature is a resource well, the implication is that humans, too, are "resources." But resources are to be calculated and used.

That such a view is now dominant, can be illustrated by the very role which theologians and philosophers find themselves in when they play their parts within the technological context. It is not unusual that humanists, particularly philosophers and religious thinkers, are part of teams which deal with the "ethical" dimensions of technology, whether in medical, engineering or business contexts. Moreover, the situation is usually so structured that the questions asked are those which can be dealt with by some version of applied ethics, almost invariably of a neo-utilitarian kind, or those which must be coherent with the contemporary versions of calculative thinking, such as risk-benefit or cost-benefit analysis.

Such involvements while not to be rejected, come too late to the scene. The religious or philosophical thinker finds the situation one in which the enframing has already occurred and not unlike the physicist in the Heideggerian interpretation, now must become the instrument by which the technological perspective is adjusted. Rather, the deeper question of technics and the human remains one about the variable possibilities of our seeing itself. And that is a question of fundamental hermeneutics. It is as old as religion and philosophy. But it has not yet been asked as thoroughly as it might be through the focus upon technics.

By taking the very materiality of technology as a focus, the argument here is one which points up the ways in which thinkers have too often arrived too late at the problems of technics. Not only do they arrive to find technologies uncontrollable (which is to say that this dystopian argument still contains a Baconian paradigm), but they also conceive of technologies too narrowly (upon a physical or "body" model, even if extended to the global scale).

There is also a hermeneutic dimension to technics which calls for a much deeper investigation. This has been suggested by changing the focus to the ways in which artifacts are used in magic and religion—and today in the very heart of the information-computer revolution. And the hermeneutic dimension is what lies within the heart of the Heideggerian inversion of the science-technology relation. Technology as a way of seeing is hermeneutic.

Here, however, we remain too often restricted to out-moded ways of thinking. For example, in much of the artificial intelligence debate and development, one finds even Medieval doctrines of analogy with their systems of analogue/homologue at work. But to conceive of the operations of a machine as "like" that of a mind in terms of similarities, is to miss what frequently is precisely the most creative and innovative. Were artificial intelligence to merely do faster what we do, it would unlikely show us anything new. Rather, precisely because it does things differently can it give us new insights into that which we investigate.

What is needed is a rigorous and phenomenological hermeneutic of technology. Such an exploration would both explore possibilities and their limits. It woud serve both to demythologize the current impasse in Baconian technics and be a search for paradigms more suited to the contemporary problems which are posed by world technology. Technology and the human are so closely intertwined that to examine one is necessarily to examine the other. In this sense a secular spirituality is necessarily a "material" spirituality in that technics must be a central theme of its inquiry.

Chapter 5

Technology, Utopia and Dystopia

Utopian and Dystopian Possibilities

Every human culture has its select stories which capture the imagination with regard to understanding ourselves. One such story often repeated and re-interpreted in Western history is that of Adam and Eve in the paradisical Garden and of their eventual expulsion. So familiar is its theme that we call it simply the Fall. But the theme is not unique to the biblical story. In many cultures there are stories which tell of a time when humans dwell and converse with the gods until such time that something goes wrong and the whole of existence is changed into what now is the case; when time is filled with hard work, ambiguity and even suffering. Humans long for a better time, sometimes long to return to the former Paradise.

From the basic, imaginative story there springs a retelling and reinterpreting with respect to every aspect. For example, with respect for the cause of the Fall, there are interpretations which lay the blame at the feet of feminine frailty (Eve takes the fruit and tempts Adam), Manichean sexuality (the primordial couple first become aware of sex in the Fall), tragic nature (the serpent is already there and fallen from Heaven,) or Gnostic knowledge (the temptation is to become as gods and know good and evil).

Why open an investigation into *technology* with such a tale? Among the causes of the fall there appears no artifact. Neither Eve nor Adam even used a stick to reach beyond their grasp to gain the forbidden fruit thereby inventing the tool as harbinger of technology. Yet if the Fall is not immediate to technology, it is by imagining across its implicit trajectory that we take account of deep seated Western and perhaps even human hopes and fears and from these we discern an immediacy of utopian and dystopian directions. I wish to take account of three such features to set the context for understanding technology in the situation of utopian and dystopian interpretations.

First, an observation which the careful interpreter needs to keep in mind. In the Garden story the situation, but not the meaning of human existence is changed from being in the Garden to the expulsion. Prior to the Fall, God commands Adam and Eve to have dominion over the Earth, to multiply, to tend the beasts and fish and till the earth. That imperative does not change with the expulsion, but it is made difficult. Childbirth comes with pain; tilling with stones and thorns; dominion with struggle. The expulsion distorts the ease with which work imaginatively would occur in the Garden, but it does not disrupt the human task.

Second, a long, though often subterranean interpretation of the origin of the fall is the theme that it was by gaining godly knowledge that humans fell. The text indicates that the kind of knowledge involved was the knowledge of good and evil, but in the later tradition of interpretation this kind of knowledge was transformed into self-conscious knowledge. To gain ascendancy over Nature by knowledge was to tempt the gods.

Third, I wish to take account of the essential structure of utopian and dystopian themes in the story of the Fall by distinguishing between *time* and *situation*. The story itself has two explicit times, the time of the Garden, a past, and the time of the present which I shall call *existential* time. To this must be added an implicit time of the future.

If, now, we take note of how these times are situated and evaluated we find that utopian time is associated with the past and an ambiguous time with the existential time of the present. This I symbolize in a field of possibilities thus:

time	past	present	future
situation	+	∿	(?)

Were time and situation to be limited to these two possibilities, what would the human hope be? Obviously, it would be a nostalgic one—how does one *return* to the Garden? But return is impossible. In the story an angel bars the way, and in life we know we cannot return even to childhood, to our past, to "good old days," all of which have irreversibly changed.

There is, instead, an implied future time which becomes ever more explicit in the biblical tradition. The future becomes the time of the Messiah, the Kingdom, a Resurrection, Heaven depending upon which context of interpretation obtains. A new symbolism is needed:

time	past	present	future
situation	+	∿	+

Much is rooted here. For example, if both past and future are utopian and essentially different from the existential present, then the condition is set for a disvaluation of the present and a new set of possibilities arise:

time	past	present	future
situation	+	–	+

Here we first see a contrast between utopian and dystopian possibilities which, in fact, became extant in a number of historical instances. In early Christian times among the hermits, interpretations arose which contrasted this world (evil) with another world and time (good) and escape from this world or hope in the other world became a dominant theme.

Nor does this shift exhaust the field of possibilities. Were I to be adequately phenomenological at this point I would display a total field and the chart would be rather long and complex. I shall not do that, but I shall display a field of relevant possibilities so that we can take account of the role of utopian and dystopian thinking prior to linking it to the question of technology. Here is such a partial field:

time	past	present	future	interpretation
situation	+	∿	+	ancient biblical
	+	–	+	hermetic christian
	+	∿	–	dystopian direction
	–	∿	+	utopian direction
	∿	∿	∿	existential direction

It is a field of pure possibilities. In taking account of this field, I have momentarily ascended to an essential or structural level but it must not be left empty or abstract. In the first instances I noted two historically extant interpretations, the ancient biblical and what I shall call the hermetic Christian, which fit the first two possibilities.

Then I added three more possible interpretations which I shall call the *dystopian*, *utopian* and *existential* directions. The directions themselves are regressivist, progressivist and essentially ambiguous. But to instantiate these possibilities, we must ask whether there are indeed interpretations which are extant historically. The answer is not hard to find.

The progressive utopian direction contains a whole family of traditions from which I shall briefly note a few. One such view might be called the tradition of scientific enlightenment. It is the view that up until the rise of modern science the world was clothed in ignorance and superstition. Once science arrived, it began to strive towards true knowledge which becomes ever more widespread and total, so that it is only a matter of time before we will unravel the secrets of everything. In its wake will follow, naturally, social progress, ease of work, and individual fulfillment, perhaps even everlasting life. The present, of course, still has a few difficulties, but these, too, will be overcome in the future. Here the direction is clearly utopian.

The utopianism of what I am calling the scientific enlightenment interpretation differs from the previous two possibilities in that the evaluation of the past situation is dramatically different than the pasts of the biblical and hermetic traditions. There is now a negative, rather than positive past and hence no nostalgia for return. The future, however, like those of the previous traditions, remains positively valued, but the progressivist feature is one which puts relatively more weight upon the future. This is no nostalgia for a past.

Another feature which, in comparison with the previous two traditions, remains ambiguous is the degree to which the past and future are *essentially* different from the existential present. In its most blatant form, scientific enlightenment interpretations remain what I shall call *eschatological*, that is, an interpretation which maintains a qualitative difference between existential time and the time of the past and future, although this feature is now at best vestigial. The "Dark Ages" of ignorance and superstition are essentially changed with the arrival of science. But the hopes of the future are distinctly eschatological in that there will be a resolution of current existential ambiguity. The resolution will come precisely by the total victory of scientific enlightenment.

We can see this same tendency in another progressivist utopian interpretation which may be called *marxist utopian*. The past is marked by exploitation, contradiction and enslavement which reaches a stage of world-consciousness in the period of the revolution, until finally after some time of struggle is resolved in the future classless society. Once again we move from a past negative to a present ambiguous to a future positive (and eschatological) resolution. As with the previous utopian direction, the difference between past and present is marked, but clearly not differentiated between a historical and non-historical time. The difference is not essential, but ambiguated. It is the future which is essentially different and thus it remains utopian and eschatological. With respect to our two variables, time and situation, and the implicit direction of interpretation, scientific enlightenment and marxist utopian views are functionally the same.

They became, along with their direction, dominant views of the nineteenth century, although not in an uncontested way. Accompanying utopian tendencies have always been reactions which exemplify dystopian directions. We can see from the table of possibilities that such dystopian directions are the inverse of utopian ones. From a past which is nostalgically valued as good, through a present which harbours bodings, towards a future which gloomily portends a kind of end, emerges the dystopian direction.

This inversion of the utopian direction, interestingly enough, often takes its shape precisely from a utopia. Thus while the optimistic progressivism of the nineteenth century was dominant, there arose a powerful Romantic movement which countered it. Here we need to take a closer look at the dynamics of utopian/dystopian views.

Extreme scientific enlightenment projections—presumptively utopian—portrayed a world which was totally rationally organized, in which all parts functioned harmoniously due to the reign of Reason. Work was diminished or, in more recent interpretations, allocated to machines. Everything was accounted for. Such a projection was both an abstraction—and hence a reduction of the complexity of things—and an idealization.

The Romantic reaction saw in this utopian projection precisely a new kind of slavery. Were everything to be rational, what becomes of feelings and emotions? Were everything ordered, what becomes of spontaneity and creativity? Were everything harmonious and predictable, what becomes of human freedom and possibility? In short, the utopia of the scientific progressivist was seen not as a hope, but as a foreclosure, a possible totalitarianism. Utopia would be, if realized, a dystopia.

With this inversion of valuation came another story as well. Contrary to the progressivist view that the past was a "dark age" filled with ignorance and superstition, the Romantic view was that in the past humans knew how to live in harmony with nature, not through rational manipulation, but through an intuitive sense of things. The invention of science-rationality–cum technology intrudes upon the scene and introduces an *artificial* element which as it increases in time ever further alienates humans from primordial Nature, until such time that the mechanical-artificial becomes the ruling factor and enslaves humans to its now reified sway. Here the dystopian direction is from the good past, through the ambiguous and danger-fraught present, to the evil foreclosure of total dystopia in the future.

Now we now have instantiated the various relevant utopian and dystopian possibilities and directions along with at least a suggestion of their dynamics. I must now turn to the way in which this field of possibilities plays upon the phenomenon of technology.

Technology in the Utopian/Dystopian Field

First, utopian themes: The Renaissance, birth age of modern science and technology, was filled with utopian dreams. These dreams—highly imaginative—approximate what today we would call science fiction. Giordano Bruno not only envisioned infinite worlds, but a virtual menagerie of beings, inventions and possibilities (and we shall not forget he was burned at the stake for his troubles). Moreover, as we locate the origins of modern science-technology in this optimistic revival of classical knowledge, we should not forget how thoroughly the era was one in which the scientific imagination took technological form.

Leonardo da Vinci's famous imaginative inventions of possible machines which anticipated submarines, helicopters, tanks, robot instruments and the like were technologically embodied concepts. Galileo's diaries reveal how much of the time he spent seeking and satisfying sponsors (and how much he hated having to teach students). These strike an anticipatory echo of today's university science establishment seeking grants and ways to have more research time.

But it is in the development of a new concept of science-technology that the utopian direction arises. That concept is that (scientific) knowledge is power, power to change the very world. Its origin is not to be linked with any one individual. For example, Nicolai Machiavelli, in his advice to the princes of his region, enunciated the notion that *technique* may be employed to political ends, a technique undertaken with strikingly modern detachedness and calculativeness. Here was knowledge as power.

Perhaps the most dramatic and utopian visions of this concept, however, come from Francis Bacon who specifically accounts for knowledge as power, as the means of overcoming human limits, of changing society, of even challenging nature. Knowledge equals power; power equals the means by which we change a world; to change a world is to exceed the bounds in which we have found ourselves. Utopia is a world which is new and changed and *good*. Knowledge-power is the means by which we deliberately leave the Garden.

Today this notion is neither novel nor strange, but we must not forget that the association between knowledge and power was not always taken for granted. Indeed, Greek classical science, in contrast to the science which emerged in the Renaissance was *contemplative*. Its aims were not to change a world, but to unite the knower with the Order of things, the human logos with the divine Logos. Any changes were at most changes within the soul. Baconian science-technology is in that sense a dramatic shift in the foundations of science such that the very conditions of life change in its application.

In contrast, if dystopian directions invert utopias, the counterpart to Bacon may well be Christopher Marlowe's "Dr. Faustus." The plot is a familiar one, a pact between the hero and the Devil, a bargain of a soul for something that is desired which lies beyond the powers of an ordinary mortal. Only in this case what is desired is precisely the knowledge-power which we have identified as the telos of science-technology. Faustus wants the power-knowledge to heal, to work wonders over the material, to exercise and manipulate events and even Nature.

When granted this knowledge-power by the Devil, Faustus at first is captivated by fascination and success, but inevitably, as things get complicated, his decline and captivity by the very causes he has let loose lead to his downfall. The very utopian hope turns out to be a temptation of the sort which leads to a Fall.

Here we have two themes which reverberate with the previous observations. There is, in Faustus, the identification of knowledge-power with the hubris of wanting to become a god, an echo of one of the Garden story possibilities. And implicitly, there is in Faustus the subterranean nostalgia for remaining intuitively placed within Nature, not exceeding its bounds. To do so tempts the gods and threatens the very position of humans. Faustus is the inversion, the dystopian underside of Baconian utopianism.

A second dystopian legend, not individually authored but arising out of medieval cabalistic thought, is the legend of the Golem. In this story, again in a quest for knowledge-power, parts of corpses are fashioned together in a reconstructed body which through a piece of word-magic is given life (the sacred and secret word is placed under the tongue of the Golem who then comes to life.) But, as with the Faust story, the creature-creation of a human takes on unpredicted powers of its own and soon becomes a threat to its own master. Creation runs out of hand and creature becomes monster. In this legend the giving of life to that which was dead becomes a theme.

Mary Shelley combines Faustian and Golem themes in what becomes the classic statement of technological dysto-pianism in her story of Frankenstein's monster. Here the mad scientist—mad because he seeks a kind of arcane knowledge which will allow him to give life to the dead and hence have power over life itself—again sews together the parts of corpses. These are endowed with life through mysterious technological machines, creating the ambiguous monster of the original story whose initially benign actions turn out to be misdirected and overpowering with respect to his creator. In short, the monster, a creation of humans, takes on its own direction which, though "designed" to be beneficent, wracks havoc in its wake. The implicit moral of the story is that things are better left alone and that humans should live within the bounds that are theirs.

I have cited these imaginative stories for two reasons here. First, in both utopian and dystopian forms, from Bacon to Frankenstein, technology as the means by which humans change things, either for good or for evil, becomes ever more the theme. Second, the elements of the stories remain the central guiding ideas in so much of the contemporary debate concerning technology that they cannot be ignored as originary in terms of hopes and fears. I turn to a very brief account of aspects of those current debates.

The contemporary field of debate over the fate of technological civilization continues to be marked by both utopian and dystopian directions. Here, at least in the larger picture, one may detect something of a shift. If the nineteenth century was dominantly utopian—progress was inevitable— the twentieth century becomes filled with doubts. It is even possible that there could be a scientific-technological negative eschaton, a destruction of the world with a bang (nuclear war) or with a whimper (global pollution leading to the greenhouse effect). Prior to the twentieth century, such *universal* global change due to human action simply was not possible. Thus while we still may find striking examples of utopian thinking, they are usually muted and more specifically limited to what I shall call *particular trajectories*. Contrarily, dystopian prophecies frequently are totalistic in scope. I shall cite a few examples of each.

A few years ago in a book destined to become both controversial and the very paradigm of critique of the computer establishment, Hubert Dreyfus described a pattern of extrapolation which I think shows very well the particular utopian projective tendency of much of the research establishment. In *What Computers Can't Do* Dreyfus argued that this pattern was one in which, from some initial success one would project an extrapolation which I shall call *vertical*, and which then points to another level entirely of attainment. But the projection overlooks levels, complexities and changes of domain.

From initial successes in the early sixties, computer utopians predicted that it would be only a short time until they would be able to (a) have a chess playing program, (b) have a translation program, and (c) be able to have forms of pattern recognition such as would allow computers to write journalistic accounts of events. Dreyfus argued that none of these aims would be achieved due to flaws in the very notion of pattern recognition and the concept of thinking. I shall not enter here the complex arguments he made, but will concentrate on the extrapolative tendency which may be found rampant in current scientific-technological utopian directions. (As it turns out, Dreyfus was wrong about the chess playing program, although probably for the right reasons. I suspect he is epistemologically correct about the difference between the way in which humans and computers "think," but he overlooked the essentially closed, and though incredibly large and complex in number, the finite sum nature of chess games thus making possible a computer program to play chess even though it took two and a half decades rather than the "few years" projected by the initial optimists. But with regard to language translation, the contextual and open-ended nature of ordinary language is such that so-called translation computers are still no more than the "mechanical dictionaries" Dreyfus predicted. Publicity hype does not change this fact. As for writing programs, I attended a conference about three years ago in which one of these programs was demonstrated, and I would have to conclude that it was, at best, a kind of mimic joke.)

Here, however, we need to note the utopian pattern, the trajectory which aims vertically without recognizing plateaus or complexities. The tendency is rampant and is often associated with justifications for some particular development. Nuclear energy is one area where this tendency went unchecked in its early days. The promise was for cheap, safe, indefinitely developable energy. Today we know that it is not cheap (uranium, like oil, has risen in costs and is not indefinitely large in supply) nor as safe as those who originally contended (Three Mile Island), nor indefinitely developable. It may not even be economically feasible.

But perhaps the most dramatic example of vertical utopian projection is the illusion created by presumably increased life span projections and the leap in level which is always implied. There is no evidence that individuals, properly cared for and in the right circumstances, live any longer today than they did in ancient times. There are and have been a few individuals who actually live into their hundreds, perhaps even to one hundred and thirty, but medical science has not been able to extend the horizon. Yet we are constantly deluged with projections which, by comparing mean age in 1600, say, with 1980, lead one to believe that everlasting life is only a matter of time. If the mean death age in 1600 was thirty-nine and in 1980 is sixty-nine, this does not mean we have solved the problem of aging, but that more people today live closer to their biological plateau than they did in 1600. Clearly this is some kind of improvement, but it is an improvement of a different order than pretended by the utopian implication. (Moreover, given this success and a changed demography where ever larger segments of the population become old people with high health and support costs, we may find the social consequences rather complex to say the least.)

In short, a regional or particular trajectory from some initial success to a utopian conclusion remains very much a part of the implicit utopianism of the scientific enlightenment. In contrast to this utopianism, however, one finds in the twentieth century a widespread phenomenon of dystopian totalism. This is so much the case that the American author, Samuel Florman, wrote a book called *The Existential Pleasures of Engineering* in an attempt to rhetorically counter this doubt.

The list of twentieth century books which could be called dystopian is rather large and I shall make reference only to a few which have been influential in the relatively new field of philosophy of technology. Jacques Ellul's *The Technological Society* and Herbert Marcuse's *One Dimensional Man* became very popular in European and North American circles in the late sixties and seventies. Both were philosophical versions of totalistic dystopian directions. Ellul argued that technology should be thought of, not so much as hardware and systems, but as a kind of analytic *technique* which becomes, in modern societies, all-embracing. Technique becomes total and hence like religious civilizations of the past, becomes the very way in which anything is considered. There is no escape from technique.

Marcuse's argument is similar in shape and he argues that the calculative society is a society on the way to closure. Once the "rationality" implicit in technological society pervades all realms, it will become totalitarian to the degree that revolution itself becomes virtually impossible. All "choices" will be simply alternatives within one dimensional society as today in consumer society "choices" are choices between brands, not between differences of kind.

Contained within both these books and echoed in many contemporary arguments, is the theme that technology has become a force which is out of control, which submits neither to individual wills nor to governmental control nor even to international control. In short, it, like the Frankenstein monster, is now plunging us into a dystopian destiny which will eventuate either in global warfare, global environmental degradation, or global totalitarianism.

Such are the utopian and dystopian projections with respect to technology as thematic focus. If a generalization may be noted, while the battles of utopianists and dystopianists have yet to be settled, there does seem to have been something of a shift in attitude from the dominant optimism of the nineteenth century to the doubtful and perhaps even dominantly pessimistic, or at least fearful attitude of the twentieth century. What this minisurvey of interpretations should have shown is that these directions of interpretation have been with us for a long time. Indeed, in certain essential respects, they have been with us since our cultural beginnings.

Such an observation is both heartening and disheartening. It is heartening because perhaps by isolating and recognizing strains of interpretation and by objectifying them, we can gain some distance upon them. It is disheartening in that by the very fact that we realize how recalcitrant they are in our cultural history, we realize how difficult it is to escape or transcend our cultural skins. But at least by placing both historical and contemporary hopes and fears concerning technology in the matrix of interpretative possibilities, we can change the set of questions concerning technology. It is to that task that I now turn.

The Phenomenon of Technology

The radical and simple way of shifting perspective would be to ask two bold questions: What is the phenomenon on technology itself? And from this "thing itself," what is the truth of utopian and dystopian interpretations? In a sense this is the way in which the phenomenological philosopher, Edmund Husserl, would have approached the problem. And, equally boldly, it is the way in which his successor, Martin Heidegger, did address the problem, particularly in his essay, "The Question Concerning Technology," in which he addresses the question, what is the *essence* of technology?

But to ask this question as boldly and directly as this simultaneously leads to the possible criticism that one believes he or she has found a privileged perspective, perhaps even one exempt from interpretative prejudices, from which to gain a view of the "things themselves." Yet the shift to a kind of phenomenological empiricism does seem to me to be necessary if we are going to distance ourselves from an eternal dynamic of the standard debates. Thus what I propose to do in this inquiry is to gradually approach the hopefully modest aim of asking: what is there in the phenomenon of actual human interactions with technology which gives rise to the current arguments? Then, from this set of observations I hope to show something about the essential possibilities of the human engagement in technology.

In undertaking this part of the inquiry, I shall employ most of the key methodological notions of a strictly governed phenomenological investigation, in particular the idea of a strict correlation between the concrete human experience of a world, i.e., intentionality, and a use of variational method, i.e., variations employed in such a way as to determine what is *invariant* (or structural or essential as the case may be).

I begin, with an imaginative exercise which, while an example of variational investigation, may be called the story of "From the Garden to the Earth." Could humans live without technology? And, if so, what would be the quality and situation of their life? Here I wish to begin with a very broad, but concrete sense of what shall count as technology, a focused but open notion which preserves such features as the materiality of a technology, its creation or invention by humans, and its incorporation into a praxis. Thus a "technology" is some artifact or set of artifacts, incorporated into a praxis in such a way that some human activity is involved and expressed.

A simple example may be imagined—the archaic human who uses a stick to knock down an ordinarily unreachable bunch of bananas is employing a "technology." He is using a material artifact to "extend" his bodily reach to attain some desired end. In this primitive act he has already taken a technological step. But could he live otherwise in a pre- or non-technological way? Empirically we may already note that humans do not live this way, but we are not simply exploring an empirical generalization. We want, instead, to examine essential possibilities. So, we must construct an imaginative example, but within the limits of the concrete.

I think, as a limit-case, the answer is yes, but such an existence would be that of a "Garden." First, because the human is mostly hairless compared to most animals, human geography would be limited to some place tropical which neither reached the extremes of hypo- or hyperthermia. Humans can populate the Earth only with clothing which is ipso facto a "technology" (material artifact employed in a praxis which transforms a situation.) Without clothes, only a Garden is possible. Second, with respect for food, the Garden would have to have an annual and plentiful supply of easily reachable, attainable and digestible food, fruit, shellfish, berries and an absence of large predators. Tools, weapons, fires, of course must be precluded if a nontechnological existence is to be maintained. Again, human habitation would be that of a Garden, not the whole Earth.

One can very rapidly see where this example leads. Only those directly bodily and expressive activities would obtain. Existence in the Garden of pretechnology must be also preliterate (writing employs transformed artifacts), face-to-face and protected by a beneficent Nature. Any changes which might occur in this environment could only be threats to the very conditions of life. Contrarily, I hope you can see, that much of what we currently believe to be human need, even "necessity," implies "technology" in some sense. To have chosen to leave the Garden and inhabit the Earth—a mythical "choice" which was made in prehistorical times by every human society—is to have "chosen" a technologically mediated existence. Today, in fact, given world population and its impact upon raw nature, it would probably be impossible to return to this new concept of Eden.

In this imaginative construction I am suggesting that, while it might be possible to live nontechnologically, it would clearly be to live within limits probably no longer possible.

Here we must turn to an even closer look at the human interaction with technology: what happens to our experience of the environment, the *world*, when we take up the very technology which allows us to inhabit the earth? In this examination I shall be employing—but without a lot of technical terms—the central notions developed in phenomenology. I shall assume that human experience is focused, is directed first outward to an experienced environment, takes place within projects which involve us in holistic fashion so that both our minds and bodies are committed, and that what results reflects back upon how we understand ourselves. All of this is implied in the complex idea of *intentionality* or what I may call the human-world interactive experience.

My first task, here, is then to distinguish between what at its limits would be a nontechnological experience of the world and a technological experience of that same world. Again variations between our story of a nontechnological experience of the world and a technological garden and the inhabitants of an earth may be instructive. I return to that simple example of the archaic human using a stick to extend bodily reach to some fruit.

Were we to look at that example closely—phenomenologically as a rigorous science of experience—we would note that there are subtle, but marked differences between picking the fruit by hand and by stick. We may note this by concentrating upon the perceptual and bodily experience involved. I shall point to only a few features which are, nevertheless suggestive of a much wider set of essential characteristic implied in our taking up technology: the hand picker of fruit engages the fruit in a full, ultrasensory experience of the object (fruit). He sees it, feels its hardness or softness, smells it and tastes it. In contrast, at least when limited to the instant of the picking, the technological picker of fruit experiences it both as mediated *through* the artifact or tool, and as limited with respect to its sensory dimensions. He may see the fruit, but in the moment of picking, does not as fully experience the softness or hardness of the fruit, nor does he yet smell it or taste it— although the ultimate aim is to bring that fruit within reach of precisely those senses. He does, however, have a bodily or kinesthetic, though transformed experience of the fruit itself in the moment of picking. He feels the resistance of the stalk through the stick itself, and, contrarily, the stick as means, not the object of experience, is not primarily experienced except as incorporated into the picker's own bodily sense. I hope you can begin to see that our simplified example turns out to be both more complex than first thought and yet filled richly with the very essential structures which mark at least one set of human-technology relations. Let us from the beginning link these to our interpretative background of utopian/dystopian directions.

The utopian fruit picker might well be the first human elated by the sense of power and attainment experienced in the extended reach which the stick gives. He is fascinated with this new ability to touch, to extend beyond his bodily limit. But simultaneously, he is not aware of, or overlooks what happens in that moment. The fruit itself, while technologically mediated, is not yet the full, multidimensional object it will be when he then picks it up by hand and devours it.

Contrarily, the dystopian, seeking to remain in the Garden, pays primary attention precisely to that sensory nearness, to that basic immediate sense of the fruit. He is temporarily satisfied with just what is there or thought to be there. But he overlooks the other kind of richness which the tool user experiences, the reach into the previously un-reachable. Thus at this simple and basic level, we can already see a potential for both utopian and dystopian interpretations. But we can also see that both are reduced focuses upon different dimensions of the human technological experience.

Before moving to the next step, let us note that this simple example also contains precisely those experiential elements which pertain essentially or invariantly, not just to archaic tools, but to even our most sophisticated contemporary technologies. The telephone, a technology much more complex than our stick, with its now worldwide connective system which includes everything from subterranean cables to satellites, when used displays the feature I have called an *amplification-reduction* structure. That is, the telephone extends our verbal reach, in this case far beyond the extended kinesthetic reach of the stick, throughout the world and we hear and are heard by another. But perceptually, as with the stick, this extension is also a reduction of our sensory experience of the other. Our experience is reduced to a mono-sensory dimension and even that is partially reduced to the still "tinny" or "phony" sound of the other's voice. Distance is diminished to a nearness, but that nearness remains the partially irreal nearness of machine mediation. Our gain is simultaneously a loss, or stated positively, we experience an essential ambiguity in our experience of what is the other through our technology.

If there is phenomenologically and essentially an ambiguous necessity involved with our experience of technology, then one could assert a thesis: careful, rigorous phenomenological analysis of the experience will show that *any and all technology is nonneutral*. And the word is chosen carefully so as not to prematurely decide that there is a dominantly good or a dominantly bad trajectory implied in technology. But there is a *nonneutral* transformational effect to any and all technology. Thus our mythical "choice" made in the new Eden is a choice fraught with significant and even dangerous consequences. To reach for the fruit technologically in order to inhabit the earth, is to step out in a way which at least historically, and perhaps ontologically is irreversible. There is no return to the Garden, yet there is a residual sense in which every action refers back to the Garden.

By the reference back to primal experience, I mean that even in our most complex and high technologies, there is the need to bring results, effects, objects within the neighborhood of human experience. To know still means in some very basic sense, "to see," to be available from a perceptual position. I shall use a very recent example from physics: the atom, hypothesized by the Greeks and multiplied into a microworld of particles by the twentieth century, has always also been sought by our desire to *see*. But only after the development of highly complex microscopic techniques—it is a long way from the first lense systems of the eleventh century to the electron microscopes of the twentieth—tied to sophisticated photographic processes that the first pictures of atoms became possible. Only two years ago some physicists at Stony Brook and Stanford claimed to have attained the first photographic representation of an atom (not a molecule, which had been photographed for some time). To see, to grasp, to eat, remains that primal base reference even in the midst of the virtual technological cocoons we utilize in the twentieth century.

Yet we are also now very far from the stick. What brought us here to the point in human history where the earth is interconnected by communications, where what were once tribal wars can now be global threats, where famine in one part of the earth may bring a response from its other side? I should now like to take a second step in this analysis of the phenomenon of technology. If the first step shows that all technology is essentially ambiguous, nonneutral, the second step shows that there is a latent trajectory to technologies such that technological directions occur which incline, though not determine human curiosity and desire.

The history of the development of lenses is illustrative. We do not know who or why the first lenses were invented, but already in eleventh century Europe they were in use. Surely one very practical and basic use was for eyeglasses, one of the earliest applications. To be able to see clearly and distinctly when before one saw only a blur has its own obvious advantage. (But we must not forget that this gain is not unambiguous—the eyeglass wearer may overlook and almost forget that what he sees is accompanied by back glare, by the intrusion of the frame and by foreshortening of the depth of field even in the best of circumstances, but these "reductions" are more than compensated for by the correction of his bodily limitations.) From eyeglasses, it is not far to greater magnification, so before the scientific revolution of the Renaissance there were magnifying glasses and even compound lens systems which eventuated in the microscope and the telescope.

These latter developments, then complex technologies, allowed that same greater magnification (and often overlooked greater reduction) of the world than ever before. Unimagined wee beasties appeared in the drops of water seen through the microscope, and mountains and valleys upon the surface of the moon. It is not hard to imagine the fascination which accompanied such inventions—and with it the temptation to project wildly ever greater extrapolations. Our engagement with our own artifacts can be one of fascination, a fascination which allows us a trajectory of development. If a little magnification yields the previously unknown, what can greater magnification give?

Here, however, I want to point up a possibly overlooked factor in our initial fascination with such technologies. Fascination can be accompanied by a forgetfulness, a forgetfulness which overlooks the essential nonneutrality which always also contains a reduction for every amplification or magnification of our experience through technology. To see the mountains of the moon through a telescope is to focus upon what might be called a microelement of the whole. To see the moon through a telescope is, while it occurs, to lose it as a part of the heavens, to enclose it within a bounded frame. It is to reduce both its sense of distance and its relations to the surrounding stars and earth. And, as with all lenses, it is to decrease its focal plane to that of a certain kind of surface.

Naturally, we can be aware of that "trade off" as we now call it. But equally, we can become reductive utopians and forget that for every gain there is a simultaneous and necessary loss. In short, we are frequently *inclined* to follow that which fascinates and forget or at least allow to be recessive what is lost. If I may be so bold as to make a generalization, I think that at least one reason why today's most prestigious fields of scientific research are in the realm of the microworld is precisely this technological inclination. Particle physics (with its enormous atom smashing tools), microbiology with gene slicing and DNA-RNA research, and even psychology with its new time-lapse tools, are following the latent trajectory of high-technology instruments.

But technology does not have its own momentum. It is created and embodied only within a human community. But possible trajectories are suggested and some of these are frightening. Here the obvious example is weapons development. The first human who killed with a club amplified his bodily strength with a technology. Later even kinesthetic distance was overcome with spears and the bow, and later still but along the same trajectory the modern aircraft with the Exocet missile which sank Britain's finest advanced destroyer was in the same destiny of extension. To have power, greater power, and power at a distance is also a trajectory which, in the case of nuclear weapons is a quantitative change which becomes a qualitative change.

Samson, however strong, might slay a thousand Philistines with the mere jawbone of an ass, but even his might is not universal in threat. With nuclear weaponry such threat of extinction is concretely universal in extent. The overkill power to extinguish twenty times rather than ten, while probably economically powerful enough to depress a worldwide economic development, does not raise the plateau of universality an iota. It is a trajectory taken to its total conclusion. I need not enter the tendency of the dystopian here, because in the face of such a trajectory, all of us may become dystopians. Yet I would remind you that the trajectory itself is latent from the beginning. It lies in the escalation of the amplificatory-reductive possibility of technology taken up. It is a burden we have "chosen."

I have now taken two steps in a phenomenology of technology. The first step points to the essential, nonneutral possibility of technology which structurally belongs to any and all technology. I have then pointed out that in our engagements with technologies, trajectories emerge, trajectories which refer back to our own imaginations and desires, but which by extending the amplificatory (and reductive) structures of technology, can actually result in qualitative changes with respect to human destiny. These are both positive and negative and often they are two sides of the very same technology.

I should like to take only one more step before drawing a conclusion. It lies in a question hinted at before: given essential ambiguity and the possibility for projecting a trajectory, does technology incline or determine our fate? It is here that we locate the very contemporary dilemma concerning technology, a dilemma which we can neither escape or dare to avoid. Once again I turn to a very simple example, variant technologies of writing.

Print, writing, or language "reduced" to writing is now at the center of much of the European philosophical interest. Speech, the language of the Garden, has become writing, the language of technologically inhabited earth. For writing is technologically mediated. But my example focuses upon precisely that writing-technology interaction. It is an example which points to the question of inclination versus determination. My variants are three technologies of writing with respect to stylistic results.

I begin with a now archaic example, writing with a dip pen or quill. In this case my experience of writing is one in which two elements emerge to suggest a trajectory for style. One is the relation between the speed of composition with respect to thought, and the other is the taking shape of the actual letters and sentences upon the page. With respect to the speed of thought compared to the writing, I find that the writing is much slower than thought. I can revise a sentence, turn it over, edit mentally, if you will, while actually writing. By the time the sentence is complete, it will hopefully be well-turned. Simultaneously, the sensuous form of the lettering can take on its own fascination. The curves and shapes can be well- or ill-formed. Handwriting is a craft or art in its own right. Perhaps these two elements even reinforce each other, for to write the visually beautiful script is to write even more slowly. And thus perhaps we discover a secret of the style of the *belle lettres*. The eighteenth century was a time when letter writing flourished (and before it the illuminated manuscript), enhanced in direction by the technology of quill or pen.

Now move to the fast electric typewriter. Here the author may now compose more rapidly, indeed, the accomplished composer can type at a speed which much more closely approximates the speed of verbal thought itself. And with respect to the letters—those are set by the ball in the machine or its keys. Editing now is not, and cannot be so simultaneous with composition. It becomes a matter of revising, retyping, redoing. My suspicion is that the inclination to style here is more journalistic, more immediate, perhaps more casual.

Then let us develop one step more, the word processor, that is the electric typewriter hooked to a visual screen which reproduces what is written, only later to be printed from a disc. Speed and shape do not change here, but editing does. In fact, from the labor of the retyping, the word processor makes editing simple. You can remove words, correct them, rearrange sentences and in fact there is something of a shift in fascination—I have a colleague who has a processor who remains fascinated with the project of rearranging (which appears on the screen like a movie in action) after two years. Whether this will result in the better written book remains to be seen, but it clearly allows the book to virtually grow in all directions at the same time. We may see the return of Germanic tomes through the word processor (and since one can easily move entire footnotes at once, probably more heavily annotated works).

My point is now this—in each case, the different technologies of writing have subtle differences of action and differences of focus with which the writer is engaged, and thus a difference of inclination concerning which style emerges easily from the differently used instruments. *But* this inclination is not in itself a determination. Not only may the writer choose his instrument, but he can go counter to the latent inclination. Verbally one could write *belles lettres* with the word processor, but the process of composition and way of attaining this style would be different, and vice versa with respect to scholarly or journalistic styles.

However, to counter the latent inclination is also to move against the center of gravity, the point of ease which the machine most clearly allows. A kind of effort must be employed or discipline or habit. Thus when a type of instrument becomes common and widely employed, and when one considers vast numbers of users, it becomes less and less likely that overall or generally this resistance of direction will be more than the exception. At the social level inclination more closely approximates determination. Thus the border between inclination and determination is itself ambiguous. But the technology itself—and we must resist reification—does not determine, although if used it may incline. It is here that we reach that fearful and yet challenging dilemma of the twentieth century.

Conclusion

I must now draw our circle to a conclusion. I began with observations about our tendencies to interpret things in a utopian or dystopian fashion, which I then contrasted with a beginning phenomenology. In the process, I hope to have shown that while both utopian and dystopian directions are not entirely fantasies—they project and extrapolate from actual essential possibilities—they are reductive of the complexity of the phenomenon. But, the phenomenology of technology, shows that our use of and choice of technology is fundamentally ambiguous. The very nonneutral structure of human-technology use is based upon the amplificatory-reductive aspects of artifact mediation. Yet, once chosen, there also emerge trajectories with latent inclinations, themselves ambiguous, but with more definable results and pathways. These pose both the promise and the threat of the twentieth century and the dilemma of technology which we simply cannot avoid.

Thus, if we return to the very first stories of interpretation and the table of possibilities, it should be clear that what emerges from this meditation is also an opting for the one unexplored interpretative possibility, the existential one. There is no Eden, and by implication there can be no Paradise, because to be historical, embodied human, is to be immersed in the essential ambiguity which we have seen to be an invariant feature of our engagement with technology.

We are tied to our own fate and responsibility. We cannot reverse ourselves to a pretechnological culture since we have already too heavily populated the earth beyond the Garden. And, indeed, by following the trajectories we have invented (and unleashed) in our technologies, we have also changed the face of the earth itself. These changes are far from trivial and the roadways, lights and even changes of the balance of Nature which can be seen while travelling the earth are real effects upon the global situation. There is a sense in which the earth, now dominated by culture as it were, while dependent upon nature, also contains nature within its bounds.

In short, at the end of this meditation, we discover what the funny little cartoon character, an opossum named Pogo, claimed: "We have met the enemy, and he is us." And we have to add: "He is us with a big stick." The dilemma of technology is the dilemma of contemporary humanity. If we cannot come to grips with ouselves—not individually, but individually and socially and politically—we *will* find ourselves in the Franken-steinian fate. Not because Frankenstein has come to life, but because we have failed to see that it is we who are still pushing the buttons which give him the semblance of life. The earth has been delivered to our care and we do not now dare avoid facing the critical ambiguity which belongs essentially to our situation.

Chapter 6

Technology and Cultural Variations

Introduction

Philosophy of technology is a recent field within academic philosophy. Its roots, as both Rapp and Ihde have shown,[1] are multiple as are its thematic questions. Historically, however, it remains the case that what is today called philosophy of technology is largely a Euro-North American discipline. It has risen at a time when it is almost impossible for critical and reflective thinkers *not* to thematize what has become a highly important factor in virtually every dimension of human life. Ours are technologically saturated cultures, and in that respect they are both qualitatively and quantitatively different from cultures which have preceded us. But the technology about which we are prone to reflect is both a scientific and industrial technology. Thus it is no accident that in the Euro-North American context there are concentrated groupings around two sets of "internal questions."

On the one side, there arises a set of internal questions related to the classical concerns of philosophy for epistemology, ontology and metaphysics. These include issues which are common to the philosophy of science and its history. For example, questions arise about how technology is related to, differs from, effects science. Euro-American philosophers inquiring into such matters include a wide range of figures— from positivistic and analytic thinkers who usually emphasize a strong difference between scientific and prescientific technologies, and who often maintain an epistemological primacy

116

to theory over practice, of science over technology. But phenomenologically oriented thinkers, most notably Heidegger, raise the same question while inverting it, making science the necessary "tool" of Technology which itself is taken as a mode of revealing a "world." In both cases, however, the very traditions of science are taken for granted.

On the other side, there arises a set of questions more relevant to ethics, social and political philosophy, which tend to focus more upon the social embodiment of contemporary technology, i.e., corporate or industrial technology. Here issues of alienation, exploitation, dehumanization, the bureau-cratization or mechanization of life, take precedence. And again the spectrum of thinkers is at least as wide as those who, on the one side, adapt a neo-utilitarian stance to create an ethical calculus to deal with medical technologies, to the other side, Marxists and Critical Theorists who deal with communi-cation, ideal languages, and questions of who benefits from technologies.

The development of such a discipline is to be applauded, particularly as it is the beginning of a critical reflection upon precisely one of the most obviously powerful of human impacts upon todays's earth. And what I have called "internal questions" are necessary to address (as I, myself, have done).[2] But there are two other types of questions which are also needed, if philosophy of technology is to become more comprehensive than it is to date.

Whole-Earth Measurements

One of these dimensions is what might be called the *global dimension*. There are many pressing questions facing us today which can only be answered globally, in terms of whole-earth measurements. For example, in earth science one such global question is whether or not the earth as a whole is cooling off or warming up? Is it headed for a new ice age? Or a greenhouse effect? The answer to this global question is of obvious import to us humans and our future. Yet, we are also aware that we do not have the means to make whole-earth measurements either with respect to spatial extent or with respect to long time records (Although with satellite instruments we are beginning to approximate the spatial measurements needed.)

Similarly, and even more urgently, we have questions of global import which arise from the proliferation of nuclear weaponry and politically destabilized economies. Is a nuclear war more likely now than previously? Does the use of "tactical" nuclear weaponry necessarily lead to global holocaust? etc. Again, we have no whole-earth means of answering such questions although the answers are urgent.

I suggest that there has been a similar global question which has been a background question in the philosophy of technology—at least often dealt with by speculative thinkers who wish to deal with contemporary technology at a global level. Is there some overwhelming or even deterministic trajectory to the development of contemporary scientific technology? Both utopian and dystopian speculators have intimated that the answer is "yes." Utopians, perhaps less dominant now than in the nineteenth century, have predicted often enough that the application of scientific technology will very soon lead us into a world of leisure, the solution of social problems, and perhaps even the literal solution to everlasting life. Dystopians, contrarily, prophesy a kind of totalitarian closure made possible by the political application of a universal technology, or else the end of the world by a "bang" of nuclear war or the "whimper" of global pollution. Many more thinkers—take Marcuse and Ellul as two—speculate that even short of the above effects, scientific technology includes the probability of a universal culture, lacking in variety, and ultimately boring if not worse.

Both utopians and dystopians share some often unstated premises: that the use of technologies is in some degree deterministic; that technologies once invented and employed, exceed the abilities of humans to "control" them, a frankenstein effect; and that as a certain kind of technology becomes worldwide, it necessarily follows that its impact will likewise be one of reducing human culture to a technological uniformity. Both utopians and dystopians presume a Technology with a capital.

Unfortunately, as with the problems of whole-earth measurements, it is not at all clear that we have the concepts or tools which would be adequate to such an assessment. Yet the questions implied in the speculation are genuinely important and even urgent. The approach I shall take here attempts a preliminary and perhaps more modest approach to these questions.

Related to the global question is another: Given the obvious fact that Western scientific and industrial technologies are now spreading globally, is the trajectory one which increasingly points to a uniform development? Or, as technologies embed in different cultures, will there be multidimensioned results? Here we reach a question similar to the one Martin Heidegger raised in his famous "Question Concerning Technology."[3] I shall position myself with respect to this paper in terms of both this philosophical tradition and a set of contemporary experiences.

First, the tradition: Heidegger's essay displays what I take to be a deep insight. Technology as a phenomenon can be better understood as a means of seeing a "world" than simply as a complex of tools used by subjects. Technologies reveal worlds. I take it that what is referred to in this insight is what I shall call *cultural embeddedness*—technologies are historico-culturally embedded and this embeddedness entails a whole view of a world, including such dimensions as space and time.

However, having adapted this Heideggerian view, I shall move away from the implicit claim of his essay. His question was: what is the essence of technology? It remains ambiguous as to whether he meant simply the essence of Western technology, whether that essence was simply a globally victorious one and hence *the* technology of our era, or whether he was addressing only our internal tradition. Whatever is the case, a recapturing of an older Husserlian technique can be readapted as a critique of the Heideggerian result. Husserl claimed that the way to establish or discover essences or invariants, was by the use of *variations*. I have increasingly come to the conclusion that variational method is, in fact, the very heart of a phenomenological inquiry, and I shall apply this method to the questions at hand. In this case the variations will be cultural ones, variations upon culturally embedded technologies and their entailments.

By drawing from history and anthropology, there appears a rich field of differing ways in which humans have embedded technologies and through them experienced worlds. Contrarily, I am offering an implicit critique of Heidegger in that if it is correct that invariants can only be demonstrated through variants, it is clear that he does not utilize variants and thus his claims concerning the essence of technology must be at least reduced in scope.

Now, the experiences: My own itinerary in philosophy of technology arose from the center of Euro-North American thinking. Moreover, what I took to be questions central to philosophy of technology arose from precisely the questions mentioned in the introduction. But within the last year and a half I have encountered situations which have made me radically rethink the context for philosophy of technology. I shall briefly recount two such occasions.

The first occasion was in Colombia, South America. In February 1982 I conducted an intensive faculty development seminar series on the philosophy of technology, which was attended by persons from some four major universities. What I had intended originally was to deal with precisely some of the questions from the "internal" set of questions mentioned, including the problem of the relation of science to technology. But by the second session it became dramatically clear to me that something was wrong with the situation. To put it briefly, I became aware that what we take for granted concerning science and science education, was simply missing in this situation. Indeed, the phenomenon "scientific technology" was there perceived simply as a unity, both "science" and its "technology" were perceived as politicocultural. Scientific technology—better scientific-industrial technology—was the expression of an alien culture in the wake of which impact could be seen threats to ways of life, cultural myths, and virtually everything relating to the Latin form of life. This is to say that the very perception or interpretation of the phenomenon was different. What I could take as an important question: the relationship of science to technology, was there seen as merely an internal and probably ultimately unimportant tinkering with an overwhelmingly powerful phenomenon which had other more immediate effects. I began to realize that just as the first-time visitor to a new land can perceive things which the native takes for granted or overlooks, so those who experience the coming of what we take for granted can perhaps see what we do not see. At the very least, whatever the past may have been, science-technology in its contemporary incarnation is a unitary phenomenon, and it is the expression of a particular culture and its world—that the Latin Americans saw more keenly than had I. Reflectively, I began to discern our own tendency to parochialism.

The second occasion was not entirely different. In this case the visit was to a group of African universities in the summer of 1982. I was particularly intrigued with what I found in the Black universities. Once again it was obvious that science-technology was simply taken as a unitary phenomenon, as an already accomplished symbiosis. Equally obvious was its appearance as the historical-cultural expression of Euro-America. And its impact was one which could be seen to impact primarily upon indigenous culture. Only in this case, contrary to the threat felt by the participants in Latin America, the impact was seen as the very way to attain a future. There was, in the Black universities I visited, a belief that by the virtual total adaptation of a technological culture, one could leap ahead into a twenty-first century culture which at the least was unlike the traditional cultures which for the students were increasingly perceived as archaic and of little interest. Indeed, the parallelism with second generation immigrant children in the United States came to mind. I think of my father's generation (second) in which there was a reflection of the old-fashioned ways of their fathers and a virtually total, almost religious belief in American progress and technology.

What emerges from both these experiences is this: Contemporary technology is perceived and interpreted differently in the Third World context. Its "internal" field, that is, its history from the Greco-European West, and its science, at least as a focal framework, is submerged. Neither are the Third Worlders aware of this context, nor ultimately interested. Instead, the perception of contemporary technology is of a cultural-political context, much like the invasion of a new people, and the response has to be one of (a) do we fight? (b) do we accept? or (c) do we adapt in part and resist in part? And in these Third World contexts, we find a rich field of possibilities precisely because of this bifurcation in what constitutes the context of the taken for granted.

Here, however, I must return to the problem raised with whole-earth measurement. How can we get hold of the cultural embeddedness of technologies? And, how can we gain some distance such that we can see both our own and variant forms of this phenomenon?

To answer this question, I propose to use a phenomenological technique drawn from variational theory to analyse
three levels of culturally embedded technologies. If there is an
essence or invariant to technologies, it is to be arrived at
through variations, and in this case variations are historicocultural ones with case histories drawn from historical and
anthropological materials. The levels I shall examine will
include (a) a high altitude look at some historical examples; (b)
a comparative look at widely variant cultures with emphasis
upon differently perceived "worlds;" and (c) then a return to
the situation of technology and its interrelation between Euro-
American and Third World cultures.

High Altitude and Technological Embeddedness

If we were to begin with a high altitude survey of the ways
in which technologies are culturally embedded, it would not
take much insight to recognize ours (Euro-American) as a
technologically saturated culture. Technologies play a role in
virtually every activity we undertake and are implicated in
both the mundane and the most intimate of our daily affairs.
Our very sexuality in increasingly mediated technologically,
whether through mundane uses of birth control or through
the life-determining techniques including artificial insemin-
ation, abortion, test-tube pregnancy transfers, or whatever.
Indeed, I dare you to find a single ordinary activity which does
not implicate and engage technologies both as individual
artifacts and as implicated systems. Who today simply urinates
in a field or wood—a most basic activity—rather we engage an
entire waste and water system, an architecture, etc., all
implicating a tie-in with our technological culture.

If ours were to be taken as one extreme end of a
continuum in terms of saturation, we would find at the other
end of the continuum only a few remaining "primitive" or
"archaic" cultures, such as a few found in South America. Note
that these societies are not without technologies. The system
of hunting which utilizes nets, bow and arrow, even
sophisticated poison systems, are technologically mediated
ways of relating to an environment—but compared to ours, we
could term this a *minimalist* technological culture.

My focus is upon the variant ways in which technologies are culturally embedded, and it is preliminarily important to note that what often is taken as a kind of linear determinism is not verified in either history or anthropology. For example, the generalization often made that certain kinds of technologies—presumably high and complex technologies—incline or even determine centralist social organizations, while simple and low technologies determine toward village or decentralized organization, does not seem to be the case.

As Lewis Mumford has shown, a society with relatively simple and low technologies may, nevertheless, be highly centrally organized and attain major feats of monumental building.[4] The Egyptian pyramids and the Mayan cities are two such examples of historicocultural variants which utilize low, simple technologies embedded in high, centralized and hierarchical cultural-political organizations. Contrarily, in today's world, decentralist tendencies are often made possible by sophisticated, complex technologies. For example, centrally located and thus easily controlled media such as newspapers, have in countries which are under revolutionary pressures, often been replaced by the virtually uncontrollable dissemination of cassette and miniature tape recorders for the propagation of nonconformist news and propaganda.

This is not to say that some particular technologies lack specific inclinational *teloi*. Current types of nuclear power systems obviously are correlatable virtually only with centralized organizations, while solar systems may be either centralized or decentralized, and wood heating is likely to be best utilized in a decentralized context.

While what I am suggesting at this high altitude level is critical of some too-quick conclusions of speculative global thinkers, it is more a warning not to overgeneralize about either Technology with the capital, or about the way technologies may be culturally embedded. Rather, I suspect that the way technologies are culturally embedded as variants, relates in a more *gestalt* fashion to human forms of life. This direction is hinted at by much of Lynn White's work. Thus the same technology may be used in quite different ways in variant cultures. The wind driven rotor was used as a prayer wheel in India, but as a windmill for power in Europe; black powder was used for fireworks and celebration in ancient China, for gunpowder in the West. Here the same technologies embed differently in variant cultures.

The situation is clearly highly complex and were we to have a table of elements which could be correlated with the possibilities, the task would be suitable for our largest computers—yet if we are to suggest what the parameters for whole-earth measurement might be, we must open the door.

Cultural Variations

To do this, I shall now descend to mid-altitude and undertake a more precise analysis of some major variables in variant cultures. Clearly not all variables can be dealt with, so I shall select a few which are nevertheless highly suggestive with respect to the problems of cultural embeddedness. In typical phenomenological fashion, I will begin with perceptual dimensions. The factors I shall examine include:

1. *Perceptual origin or bodily position.* While bodily position is in a primary role with respect to first person perception, its role differs widely with respect to where it fits into our dimensions of technology and cultural embeddedness. Yet, in some primitive sense, bodily position is the point-zero from which perception takes place.

2. *Perspective or privileged point-of-view.* Related to perceptual origin, but not reducible to it, is the position from which a perspective may be taken. While there is usually a hypothetical position implied in all perspectives, it is not always equitable with bodily position.

3. *Space-time horizons.* Space-time horizons are particular interpretations of perceptual gestalts. Here I am taking a phenomenological "Einsteinian" stance which, in effect, does not conceive of space-time as a Newtonian empty and absolute container, but instead takes space-time as some configuration of material interrelations and thus for our purposes a type of perceptual gestalt.

I may illustrate how these variables work by drawing briefly from the example I elaborated at the last German-American philosophy of technology conference: Then I elaborated the vast difference between European and Polynesian systems of long distance spatial orientation, i.e., navigation. At that time I was primarily concerned to demonstrate that a technologically mediated (instrument utilization in a mathematical interpretation) and a perceptually read system varied. In that case I contended that Westerners, from the beginning, presumed a technological relation to the world, mathematically contexted, while Polynesians a perceptually direct, but hermeneutic or "read" relation to the world as means of long-range orientation.

In this context I can be even more specific with respect to the variables mentioned. First, I shall discuss perceptual origin and perspective. In the case of Micronesian navigation, as Thomas Gladwyn has so elegantly shown,[5] bodily position and perspective are identical. Even I did not realize how radical such a position would be with respect to our taken-for-granted gestalt until recently. The navigator in this system quite literally takes his actual bodily position as the fixed variable for navigation. Thus even the interpretation of primary perception takes on a sense different from our usual intuitions.

The boat does not "move through the water" as we might say—which from our set of questions now may be seen to imply a perspective *other* than that which we actually occupy— but, rather, that the island being sought moves toward the navigator, or, more immediately, the water moves past the boat as the ocean moves in relation to the boat.

The space-time horizon, then, is in motion with respect to the fixity of the navigator. Location is arrived at by noting such phenomena as "ghost islands" which are reference directions in this system of navigation that utilizes a kind of bodily geometry, but not a mathematical geometry.

Contrarily, we ordinarily think of ourselves as moving toward a point on a map, for in effect, we have separated bodily position from privileged perspective. Were we to occupy the perspective which we assume, we would be, for example, in a satellite above the ocean upon which we are moving, a "bird's-eye" perspective which indeed became the privileged perspective for our long-range orientation.

Our space-time horizon is interpreted from the fixed heavenly or bird's-eye position which is fixed while we move on the surface of the earth. This, in turn is interpreted as position on a grid of coordinates which imaginarily covers the surface of the earth.

Note that the immediate perceptual phenomena, an

example of which is the boat in the water, can make equal sense—I shall say *multistable sense*—in both cases. Here we have an "Einsteinian" relativity of perspectives: were the situation to be one of a canoe in a river with a current, it might be immobile with respect to the shore, moving with respect to the current, and could be said to be either moving against the stream or not moving with respect to the land. Both are correct, but relative to the point of variable from which the observation is made.

A.T. Aveni, an astronomer-anthropologist at Colgate University, has taken this same notion into the area of archeoastronomy which is the discipline which tries to understand and reconstruct ancient systems of astronomy. In a brilliant article, "Tropical Archeoastronomy,"[6] Aveni shows that observations of the heavens in tropical as contrasted with temperate regions are quite different. Star paths are, for instance, widely variant. In tropical regions stars traverse the heavens basically vertically from the horizon and set in the same fashion. This movement makes what Westerners call a "sidereal compass" a useful reference point (and this technique is deeply engrained in South Pacific navigation as well). Contrarily, in temperate regions which are north by virtue of the earth's land masses, star paths may be fixed (Polaris or the North Star), elliptical (above the poles), or vertical (near the equator). Thus the actual observable movements are different from the two different bodily positions of peoples observing the heavenly bodies. Aveni was able to show that there was a similarity of astronomical concepts throughout the tropical world which varied from those of the temperate world. Tropical systems use a "horizon" or sidereal system, while temperate systems employ a "polar" reference plane.

Tropical systems, for example, pay little attention to equatorial or ecliptic references, but all seem to have some version of cardinal directions from the horizon (sidereal compass), in fact with an amazing similarity of interpretation regarding pillars or ridge poles reaching into the sky.[7] This domestication of the horizon as a place of dwelling also reveals something about the familiarity with the earth and ocean included in archaic culture. A curiosity emerges when, in fact, our instruments are introduced into this scene. The Puluwati, for example, now use the compass as a steering device, substituting its ease for the finer observations needed to read wave patterns. But its circularity and the evenly divided segments posed no problems for this people who considered the earth to be square and the guide stars on the horizontal points unevenly distributed. This is because each of these elements are used for direction relative to the navigator, and neither for distance nor world-mapping—the result is equivalent or multistable regardless of whether the earth is round or square. Indeed, if the perspective and bodily position are identical, and you are situated at the same level as the horizon, the observation could be of a circle, a square or a polygon—only if you assume as outside or above or birdseye perspective does this interpretation get called into question.

In ancient astronomy a similar observation may be made in that all heavenly bodies are frequently regarded to be equidistant from the earth (as holes in the heavenly dome, for example) or, if arranged in concentric circles of distance usually so arranged in terms of some cultural set of values.

Two additional items are worth noting here: first, our tendency is naturally one which tries to bring what is radically different for us into our familiar world—thus even Aveni speaks of "star compasses" and the like, which in effect read our technologically embedded techniques into those of peoples who do not read things this way. And, second, we should note that contemporary, scientific astronomy does not in a fundamental sense belong to either of these archaic systems. In that regard it may be well to note that ours is, with respect to perceptual origin and perspective, thoroughly "Einsteinian" in that it is not even possible without a multiplicity of relative perspectives (from earth, from the sun, from our galaxy, and so forth.)

The contemporary astronomical system may be related to the three variables here as well. First, bodily position or origin of perception is at most "accidental" or arbitrary—it happens to be where I am. But even this is not often the case in a full technologized instrumental context. Much astronomy is done photographically, or through radio telescopy, frequently automated. Thus the actual activity of the observer is distinct from the instrumental use in many cases. Second, as already noted in Western navigation, the emergence of a disembodied or imaginary perspective, often privileged as more important than bodily position, is here taken one step further. Actual observations from satellites or imagined perspectives from some distant point in the universe are the norm for contemporary astronomy. Finally, even the space-time dimensions of such an astronomy become relativized and representation may take the shape of a two-dimensional representation of a "flattened" universe, a three-dimensional "Newtonian" container as with models of solar systems; or "curved" Einsteinian space as represented by computer projective representations.

Analysis of Variations

Although I have more suggested than developed the examples, I can now turn to a preliminary set of comparisons between three different cultural contexts with respect to the three variables introduced. The first group I shall call the *embodied set*. This set is illustrated in the archaic tropical astronomical and navigational systems. In this context bodily position and perspective are merged, either explicitly or implicitly. Now what this context grasps is a very fundamental and primitive experience: *I am my body*. And at this fundamental level, I may say that I experience the world from this "being-here" of bodily existence. The interpretation of space-time which is associated with this observational position and perspective can be and is coherent, orderly and while relative not "subjective." There is also a sense in which this cultural context is one in which the world is "Aristotelian" in that it is made up of concrete material individuals (sun, moon, stars, etc.) and direction is taken from these.

In the second cultural context, which I shall call the *disembodied set*, bodily position and perspective are separated. Indeed, the separation is such that a nonoccupied or hypothetical position is frequently given privileged status, usually in the form of some version of a bird's-eye perspective. Thus in both European navigation and in temperate area astronomy, an emphasis emerges upon what may be attained through a fixed, disembodied perspective. Associated with this context is what one might call a "platonic" world in that hypothetical dimension becomes the most important for the interpretation of space-time. The world-as-grid (the imaginary longitudinal and latitudinal lines on maps and globes) becomes the most important for locating the "accidental" location of our bodies. Space-time here anticipates what becomes the Newtonian universe which, historically, comes much later than its phenomenological position which was latent from the beginning.

But I have also suggested that contemporary astronomy (although not so much navigation) differs from both the previous sets in that at least implicitly it is multiperspectival. What is seen of the universe is relative to the perspective from which it is viewed. Thus only very recently have we come to understand that our very galaxy is four-armed and that we are located slightly above the equatorial mean of the Orion Arm.

While there remains, within what I am calling this Einsteinian context, a persistent use of the disembodied perspective, its very relativity recalls something of the embodied emphasis of the tropical context. The multiplicity of perspectives possible in contemporary astronomy—increasingly made materially possible by space technology and thus no longer merely imaginary—nevertheless also increasingly take account of the need for recognizing the position of the observation. Embodiment returns to the Einsteinian context precisely in the multiplicity of perspectives. Thus contrary to the possibility of taking bodily position as purely arbitrary, while not returning to the unity of position and perspective, the Einsteinian context is one which takes seriously whatever implied position and perspective is taken. We have here something like a phenomenological ascent in which the multiplicity of profiles begins to suggest something like a structure to the object of inquiry, but a structure arrived at by multiplying perspectives.

We have, then, three variations upon our variables of bodily position, perspective and space-time interpretation. But at this point it may seem that we are distant from culturally embedded technologies. I suggest, however, that this is not the case, for associated with each of these cultural sets are particular technologies (or lack of same) and particular uses which correspond to the points analyzed. One thing distinctive about Pacific navigation was in fact the absence of instruments. Waves, bird flights, stars, reflections in the sky, etc. are directly and perceptually read—a kind of body to earth-sea relation. The importance of this for the embodied context becomes apparent with the subsequent introduction of Western instrumentation.

The compass, recently introduced, is now a fairly common fixture upon sailing canoes, although it is used differently than by European navigators. We already noted that tropical space-time interpretation is not polar, and this remains the case with their use of the compass—that its needle points north/south is not a matter of importance for Puluwatians, only that it is a relative constant. Because it is easy to read; less affected by local conditions (such as storms which temporarily disrupt wave patterns), it "distances" and makes easier the task of steering. It lacks its role in a context of world-as-grid. But is very like the steel axe which is so easily accepted by stone age cultures unaware that it is not just an object, but a whole complex of intercultural relations. The compass makes for easy function and for the introduction of a new kind of distance. It transforms a perceptual context. But at this level, the instrument only inclines in a direction and does not determine it.

Tropical astronomy does utilize instruments—but curiously they remain "Aristotelian" in that they are specifically and purposely attuned to specific natural phenomena. South America abounds with "telescopes" which are permanently fixed for the locating of solstice or equinox. These are hollow tunnels built, for example, into tombs or monumental buildings, which allow the light of the sun at the right moment to shine on some particular designated spot. They are permanently fixed, single purpose instruments. Yet even here, they implicitly point to a geometrizing of the world.

As annual cycles are noted and accumulated, measurement of more and more phenomena lead to the sophisticated astronomical and calendrical systems, for example of the Maya. The material record and the material instrument display the possibility of a world instrumentally ordered. The instrument makes possible a different relation to space-time. Micronesian navigators do utilize imaginary or hypothetical entities in certain conditions. One such example is the use of "ghost islands" which, interestingly, may be considered to be points on the sidereal horizon from which to determine relative position (similarly, some parts of the sky are less populated with stars than others and this poses a problem for a strictly "Aristotelian" system). But the instrument, which may be divided equally into points, does not have this uneven but real distribution. Note that the instrument, then, transforms the *perceptual* situation in that *it* rather than the stars may be read. It distances from natural objects, but it becomes itself a perceived object to which and through which one may be located. Here, implicitly, is also a change of what counts as world. And, here, we achieve a first suggestion of variant cultural embeddedness of technologies.

The Einsteinian context is one which arose well after the rise of contemporary instrumentation. It entered history only after there was a technologically saturated culture. And I suspect that its multiplicity of perspectives with the associated accounting for the position from which the observation is taken, relates to another aspect of the human experience of technology. In the Einsteinian context the use of instrumentation is familiar, integral to scientific investigation itself, and experiences the technology as a kind of extended embodiment. The astronomer here sees *through* the instrumentation and, given the contemporary variety of instruments (telescope, spectrascope, space vehicles, satellites, etc.) the embodiments, too, are different. The multiplicity of perspectives is in this sense a familiar and taken for granted result of the mode of investigation.

At this stage, then, we have three different cultural contexts which also may be seen to be associated with three different technological complexes. So far, we may interpret each as a variant. But are there invariant features? And, further, are there detectable developmental features which may be derived from these variants?

Allow now a somewhat speculative turn with respect to technological embeddedness. If the embodied context is one which most easily associates with a direct perceptual reading of natural phenomena, what happens with the introduction of perceptual-mediating instruments? I have suggested that what first occurs is a kind of transforming distantiation. The instrument may both be read (as object) and read through (as extended sense). But this possibility is ambiguous and multistable. On its one side the instrument as object is other then me and that to which I must relate; on the other, it extends or amplifies my capacities such that it is partially *embodied*.[8]

Now my speculation is this: first or early uses of instruments must be learned. Before being embodied, they must be mastered and often that task is difficult. Take the automobile as an example: Most of us are so accustomed to driving that it is a kind of second nature—indeed, we pay little attention to the action, yet entailed in this embodiment of motion through the car is a good deal of familiarity with the car's capacities, traits, etc. Now feature the following situation, common to countries in which cars are used. A driver becomes a bit inebriated and, upon taking the wheel with both diminished senses and perhaps too extended sense of his ability to drive, soon is exceeding the speed limit. He comes to a curve, too fast, and the result is an accident easily explained in physicist's terms. Now imagine the two following reports: (a) "I guess I had too much to drink. In any case I got to the curve and found I was going too fast and lost control of the car. I ended up in the ditch." Or (b), "I had been to a party and had a few drinks. When I got in the car I headed it home, but when the curve in the road came up, the car, it had its own idea, and I could do nothing with it. It drove itself off the road and wrecked me." In both cases the loss of control describes correctly what happens when the inertial force exceeds the friction and center of gravity for the car to be under control. But in one case the driver sees the situation as one of losing control; in the other the driver sees the car as taking on its own character. One description begins from an embodied experience of the car; the other from a more disembodied or otherness experience of the car. Now these two descriptions were, in fact, made by persons from two different cultures, with the second coming from an indigenous person for whom cars are clearly relatively new to use.

What I am suggesting is this: Both between cultures and within a culture, early experiences of new technologies are likely to have heightened ambiguous results. A given technology may be both experienced as object tending toward the alien and/or experienced as tending toward a familiar embodiment. For example, in our culture the computer may be very differently experienced by those unfamiliar with it—I sometimes conduct seminars for parents with computer anxieties for themselves and their children—and by those familiar with it. Today's "hackers" are perhaps good examples of persons who have domesticated the computer under a new metaphor: *world as game.*

But even more, when new and especially complex technologies are introduced into variant cultures, the tendency is almost inevitably one of the alien side of the ambiguity. Here, finally, we return to cultural variants, and the Third World experience.

Third World and Technological Accommodation

Third world cultures, unlike the archaic examples used above, are contemporary cultures in which the expansion of Western science-technology is clearly directly experienced. I return here to the perception and interpretation of this impact. I noted that there is a tendency in the Third World context to see (a) science-technology as a unitary phenomenon, (b) as the expression of an alien culture, and to (c) experience a struggle with respect to some mode of accommodation which cannot be avoided.

In the first place, it may now appear that the perceptions of the unitary nature of the phenomenon are in fact true. Technologies are integrated into the type of knowledge or science utilized in the culture. Our science is embodied in a complex technology and is not even possible without it. But different complexes of technologies entail different interpretations of worlds. Second, the recognition of this fact speaks for the accuracy of the second perception as well. Western science-technology is a cultural expression, albeit a now highly powerful one. And, just as a steel axe entails a gestalt of dependency and interdependency relations, so today's high technology components entail similar gestalts. Only now our previously archaic cultures recognize this.

At a second level, one might speculatively note that perhaps some of the problem in technology transfer occurs developmentally. To move from areas of experience previously embedding no technologies, into those which now do entail technologies, calls for a massive cultural shift. This is dramatically the case with those technologies which entail intimate relations, for example, birth control. While there are some minimal techniques (not technologies) of child spacing— for example long lactation periods—many cultures still do not use and resist the use of technologies in this dimension of life. And here one can see dramatically how one change entails an entire gestalt: relations between women and men, kinship relations, values, hierarchies, and so forth.

At other levels, where technologies have been employed but where new technologies are introduced, there is a shift as well. The snowmobile and the rifle have dramatically changed Eskimo ways of life, yet the adaptation to shooting was a relatively easy one to make. There is also the problem of the essentially ambiguity involved in learning the use of a technology. The multistability which allows a drift either toward a familiar embodiment, or towards a partially alienated otherness, is also sometimes culturally relative.

And at an even higher level, the movement and introduction of new technologies points to a kind of invariant which is itself cross-cultural. Here the example of computerization is a good one. The movement to a high-tech, computerized industrial complex is itself empirically virtually universal. And the problems which can be recognized in its wake, while differing in degree, are not totally dissimilar between the Third World and Euro-America. Probably the *telos* of computerization is such that it entails simultaneously low intense labor and high technical skills. The impact of such a movement upon countries where labor is both unskilled and lacking in intensity is obvious—but the same relation to the new style of unemployment in the United States can also be discerned.

It is, however, too early to make a telling prediction concerning the outcome of this movement, precisely because the technology itself is not yet part of the taken-for-granted way in which we may be embodied. We remain at the stage of fascination and lack the critical distance and familiarity to note just how dumb (or smart) this machine may be. We cannot even tell very well what uses are appropriate and what not. Although increasing numbers of people are beginning to learn about limitations and even debilities. Everyone experiences "the computer is down" as a delay to activity, and who can doubt that bank lines and transactions as well as those of ordinary sales transactions are today slower and more complicated than before? I shall never forget the prophetic memo passed around some years ago within the university which stated that we now must order our next semester's books at least four weeks earlier than previously because the ordering system was now computerized.

Contrarily, calculators have made our bookwork easier and my colleagues seem to love their word processors (as their tomes grow more Germanic by the day). Someday, hopefully, we will begin to learn appropriate uses for this machinery, although what uses these may be cannot be predicted.

Conclusion

What, then, is the moral of the story? Four things seem obvious. First, different cultures develop different technologies and uses of technology with respect to wider aspects of life forms. Negatively, technologies *per se* do not determine a form of life as such. Cultures with minimalist technologies and yet maximal centralist tendencies are possible, and vice-versa (at least in theory). In this respect technologies correlate with cultural outlooks.

But, neither are technologies neutral. Steel axes and compasses, unknown to their new users, allow different sets of habits to develop even if the artifact is not used in the same way it was in the donor culture. Thus the practice of wave-reading in Micronesia has declined in recent times and with it an erosion of an important element in perceptual navigation. Technologies incline when embedded in cultures.

Third, at virtually every stage of the development, use and adaptation of technologies, there is also an essential ambiguity or multistability possible for each technology. Any single technology can be used in ways not "intended"—this is the case for Heidegger. Heidegger's hammer, which can be used as a hammer, a paperweight, a murder weapon, or an art object—as well as for the computer network which can be used to convey money, keep book, or as a secret code for hackers to penetrate. Moreover, there are both embodiment possibilities (the car extends my bodily capacities and mobility) and objectifying possibilities (the car is "other," with alien personality).

Fourth, beyond variability, there are also stages in the adaptation and use of technologies as they are learned and made familiar. Early stages seem to entail fascination and fear and never reveal uses or consequences. Moreover, the fascination-fear stage is one which seldom reveals the limitations of the technologies involved. (I suspect that is where we are with respect to the computer as suggested.)

Where, then, does this leave us with respect to the global questions raised at the introduction? The answer has two sides, the first of which is cautionary. Given the multiplicity of possibilities, it is clearly premature to conclude that contemporary technology can or is leading humankind to a single cultural form. To answer that question one would need to know just how strong inclinatory directions are within the multiplicity of technologies we have developed may be.

Positively, it does seem clear that the empirical spread of contemporary technology is such that whatever variation there will be, will be one which utilizes a multiplicity of technologies—in short, in the clash and confrontation of cultures I see little evidence of trajectories toward minimalist forms. This is not to say that alongside the dominant cultural direction there might not be minimalist islands, just as in the nineteenth century industrialization there arose multiple sectarian revivals such as the Amish, the Amana Community and other forms of variation from the then current technological development.

Finally, our destiny clearly is tied to current technological trajectories. And while I have argued that we do not yet have anything like a whole-earth assessment of these trajectories, insofar as we are aware of this destiny, our task remains one of a most urgent need to inquire more deeply into technology and its cultural embeddedness.

Part III
Critical Essays

Chapter 7

Ortega y Gassett and Phenomenology

Ortega's centennial was in 1983. He was clearly the individual who more than anyone else introduced phenomenology to the Spanish-speaking world. But a question arises—in part from his own claims to have anticipated the ideas of Husserl and particularly Heidegger—as to his own adaptation of phenomenology. What I shall undertake in this retrospective is a rather old philosophical ploy. I shall apply some Ortega to Ortega, particularly rhetorically although obviously without the Spanish flair inherent in his own work. For this is at best an "imitation" of tauromachy by one who grew up, not as a Spanish aristocrat, but as a Kansas farmboy. But then farmboys have experience of bulls, too, although the life of a bull on the plains is very different from that of the ring—although in the end the fate is the same for both (hamburger).

Ortega as Intellectual Picador

I begin with an experience: A little over a year ago I had my first taste of Latin America with a trip to Bogota, Colombia. On the first Sunday there I decided that I should see my first bullfight, that paradigm Spanish sport which encapsulates so much of the old traditions. The pageantry was all that one could expect. Surrounding the arena were the venders and hawkers, with the spectators—which begin early filling their stomachs and wine skins prior to entry. Once

137

inside, seated on the first row, thanks to a newspaper editor's kindness, I could see everything close up. The band played classical bullfight marches; the medievally clad horses pranced; the picadors strutted, the matador was cheered; and, finally, after much preliminary, the bull entered, black and fearsome.

The bull charged around the ring, chasing the picadors and horses, until he found his spot. Then tauromachy began in earnest. *The first to draw blood is the picador.* His beribboned banderillas, long at first, then shorter and shorter ones, are plunged into the back of the bull—but they do not conceal the blood which begins to flow. I saw, eventually, the first bull killed on the other side of the ring, killed by the matador.

Variants upon the killing took place, eventually the third bull was pierced by the curved sword of the matador not ten feet in front of me. And by this time I discovered that my "circumstance," as Ortega would call my historical-cultural situation, was quite distant to the action of the ring. Indeed, after seeing now for the third time the way the picadors tormented and weakened the bull before its final solution, I turned in disgust and left, satisfied that *once* I had seen a bullfight, but enough.

What would Ortega have thought? There is little doubt. For while he was the editor of a newspaper, *El Sol*, which deliberately scorned news of bullfights, Ortega himself was an *aficionado*. And as Ferrater-Mora points out in his introduction to Ortega, "He frankly loathed (those) who showed more concern for the misery of the bulls than the agonies of the bull-fighters."[1] Had I not, during the second fight when the matador was briefly knocked down, found myself almost cheering for the bull? Ortega, on the other hand, once contemplated writing a book to be called *Paquiro or About Bull Fighting*, in which he would discuss the "dramatic relationship which has existed for two thousand years between the Spaniard and the bull."[2]

I here, however, characterize Ortega as an intellectual picador, not matador. This for three reasons: the picador is the first to draw blood; the picador torments the bull with repeated jabs which draw more blood; but the picador does not kill the bull, the matador does that, and without drawing blood until the kill itself.

What I had never grasped about bullfighting, until seeing

it in the flesh, is how much braggadocio there is to the fight. The picadors and matadors strut; they thrust their pelvises toward the bull as if to say "mine is bigger than yours"; and their costumes are both colorful and highly crafted. Posturing is of the essence, without it the ritual would not be what it is. So, for one so far from this circumstance, must Ortega appear.

The bullfight metaphor here applies to philosophical style. To give you a sense of the intellectual tauromach, I cite a few of the pelvic thrusting pronouncements which pepper Ortega's writing:

He does not spare anyone—in a sarcastic turn upon a fellow Spaniard, "Among the comic things in Spain's unfortunate intellectual life during the past century should be included the fact that Menendez Pelayo would have considered it a great triumph to move in the maturity of Scholasticism to the Scotch philosophy of common sense; this was as though one decided to leave little Malága in order to move into big Malága."[3] Similar pronouncements fill Ortega's works, including his most serious ones.

In the major work, *The Idea of Principle in Leibniz and the Evolution of Deductive Theory*, on French existentialism:

> The reader will note that by its mere *facies*, by its physiognomy, existentialism belongs to a style of life prevailing a quarter of a century ago. . . . But it has taken all this time to reach the province that Paris has been since the beginning of the century—a most curious case in which a 'world capital' has evolved into a village and consequently now exploited it.[4]

But when Ortega turns to Heidegger, the pronouncement turns to invective:

> It is inconceivable that in a book entitled *Being and Time* which claims to 'destroy the history of Philosophy,' in a book, then, composed by a tonsured and furious Samson, not the slightest light is cast on what 'Being' means, and on the other hand, this term comes to us modulated in innumerable flute-like variations: such as *Seinssinn*, 'sense of Being'; such as *Seinsweise*, 'manner of Being' . . . . and so on.[5]

or again:

This led Heidegger to what he considers a 'fundamental distinction; between the 'ontological' and the 'ontic' which, far from being fundamental, is trivial and worn out, or is an unverifiable distinction which can hardly be maintained today. But it has served those little people in all the crowded lower intellectual quarters of the world so that they can gargle with it and gain great faith in themselves—being always disposed like the ostrich to swallow lime, jewels and rough pieces of marble indiscriminately.[6]

Nor, like the tauromach, is Ortega accusable of humility. In addition to the numerous self-references—his "see my _____ " references increase with every new publication—he notes as early as 1934 in his Preface to Germans:

Germany does not know that I and *virtually I alone* have won for her, the enthusiasm of Spain . . . And something more besides. In the process I have imbued all South America with things German. In that continent across the ocean this has been freely admitted with fervor and solemnity. But Germany is unaware of this, and in Spain, where everyone knows, they have kept it to themselves.[7]

Nor is he bashful about his accomplishments:

But—the reader will say—didn't you tell us you studied at Marburg? Yes, reader, it is true. I studied at Marburg, and at Leipzig and at Berlin. I studied deeply, orgiastically, and to the very limits of my being . . . . I have argued Kant and Parmenides with Nicolai Hartmann, with Paul Scheffer (etc.) . . . Then for years and years afterward I was enthralled by German science until I almost drowned. In some of these sciences I am familiar with virtually everything done in Germany, both important and unimportant, and, since I have a fair memory, when I meet even a fifth or sixth-rate scientist I can usually recall the title of one of his works tucked away years ago in the corner of some journal.[8]

Even taking into account the tongue-in-cheek tone, the posturing takes on more serious bite in the Leibniz book:

To think that for more than 30 years—it is quickly said—I had, day after day, to endure *in silence, never broken,* when many pseudo-intellectuals of my country disqualified my ideas because I 'wrote only in metaphors,' they said. This made them conclude and proclaim triumphantly that my writings were not philosophy. It is clear that fortunately they were not, if philosophy is something that they have the capacity to set aside. Certainly, I carried to an extreme the hiding of the definitive dialectical musculature of my thought, as nature takes care to cover fiber, nerve and tendon with the ectodermic literature of the skin . . . No one had made the generous observation, which is also irrefutable, that in [my works] it is not a matter of something given as philosophy which turns out to be literature, but on the contrary, of something presented as literature which results in philosophy. But those people who have no understanding of anything understand less than nothing of beauty or style, and do not conceive that a life and a work can cherish this virtue.[9]

Here, then, is our intellectual picador, taunting, gesturing and stabbing at the bull. But a picador is also the person who draws first blood. In this case the "blood" in question is Ortega's relationship to phenomenology. He claims—and his more loyal followers and interpreters allow—that it was he who first turned phenomenology into an existential phenomenology; that it was Ortega who in effect anticipated the directions later taken by Heidegger.

In the next section I will examine in greater detail Ortega's relationship with phenomenologists and phenomenology, but first I do want to note one thing about our picador. He falters as he plunges his first banderilla into the bull. He fails to put his first ideas into print (although intimations of his critique of Husserlian consciousness were written). This is what he says about the drawing of first blood:

There are many reasons why I did not allow those ideas to be put into print at that time, and I would have to recount the life of an idea man who is *independent* and interested in improving the culture of his fellow-countrymen. But I can now state one of those reasons, because it is quickly said, so that the young who tomorrow will *set themselves to thinking* may not commit the same error that I did. This reason for my silence was purely and simply . . . timidity.[10]

Now, I ask: of a man who writes eleven volumes of *Obras Completas* in his life, and an intellectual picador whose style is there from the beginning, does it seem likely that timidity is one of his virtues?

In Ortega scholarship, the issue of first blood is crucial to the claims of Ortega vis-a-vis Heidegger. What I find in broad terms is this: There is evidence that from the outset Ortega was critical of the Husserlian notion of consciousness. Eventually, Ortega replaced this concept with that of human life, *vivencia*, which clearly carries the existential overtones at least compatible with Heidegger's notion of Dasein. Thus there is a sense in which Ortega and Heidegger might be said to have been on a similar trajectory. But I do not find in Ortega much more than this compatible trajectory compared to Heidegger. What I do find is a growing jealousy on Ortega's part with respect to Heidegger's then growing reputation.

This jealousy is clearly enough present in some of the quotations just cited. What might be missed in uncontexted citations, however, is the biographical and historical development. The most vehement invective concerning Heidegger on Ortega's part is to be found in his *later* writings. The *Leibniz* quotations are from the forties, when Ortega is already in his sixties. This contrasts to what he has to say in his 1929 lectures, *What is Philosophy?* "For that reason, I am glad to recognize that the man who has gone deepest into the analysis of life is the German philosopher, Martin Heidegger."[11] This was two years after the publication of *Being and Time*, specific themes from which are echoed in Ortega's lectures of the time. Do not forget that Ortega was six years Heidegger's senior nor that from his earlier successes in Germany, Ortega was later eclipsed by Heidegger. Here, psychologically, I think we find some of the clue to the Ortega-Heidegger rivalry.

The best insight into this situation was, for me, provided by Thomas Mermall who observed that Ortega—perhaps not out of keeping with his personality and cultural roots—had great intuitions. But these intuitions were not always and maybe only rarely followed through upon. To have intimated something is not yet to have *said* it, and certainly is not to have said it fully, systematically and architectonically. There is nothing I have found in the Ortega corpus which compares on that score with *Being and Time* (which may be, parenthetically, architectonically Germanic in contrast). Picadors draw first blood; they do not kill the bull.

Is this to be unfair to Ortega? In one sense, yes, because his project is different. But it is an unfairness which is invited by Ortega himself and by something which, I believe, is subtly essential to the situation. First, it is obviously Ortega himself whose invective stimulates the counter-barb. He who opens with rhetorical insult invites the same upon himself—that is a simple existentialist universalization. Second, it is Ortega himself who invites the comparison with Heidegger and other related thinkers. But—and here we begin to point to the deeper issue—in so doing we may in fact miss a more fundamental phenomenon. Might we not miss what is unique to Ortega, and might it not be something which while on a trajectory compatible with Heidegger's is also different?

There is yet another sense in which Ortega is an intellectual tauromach. The "two thousand year" drama between Spaniards and bulls is also deeply *Spanish*. Ortega, more than most philosophers, was deeply aware of his cultural embeddedness. His eventual existential universal, *man and his circumstance*, was instantiated first as Spanish. He self-confessedly claimed to write for Spaniards.

His first book was *Meditations on Quixote*, 1913, just after his discovery of Husserl. In it, in addition to the introduction to his "existential" interpretation of a kind of phenomenology, Ortega also introduces his own more literary approach in the form of meditations and a series of short topics. This approach remains the case even in the more didactic *Leibniz* book, 1947.

Quixote, however, is crucial. Here he introduces his notion of *man and his circumstances*, Ortega's version of being-in-the-world (prior to Heidegger), in which he sees himself embedded in a historical culture. He says, "I am myself plus my circumstance, and if I do not save it, I cannot save myself."[12] That circumstance is, for Ortega, deeply Spanish, and he is self-aware that he launches his own quixotic search from there: "My natural exit toward the universe is through the mountain passes of the Guadarrama or the plain of Ontigola. This sector of circumstantial reality forms the other half of my person; only through it can I integrate myself and be fully myself."[13]

What is human is circumstantially situated, our being-in-the-world, is culturally embedded, but this does not prevent Ortega from ambivalence with respect to that circumstance.

As philosopher he is critical and with respect to Spanish culture he evidences a love-hate relationship. On the one side and towards Spanish culture, Ortega applies his barbed rhetoric over and over again: "We Spaniards offer life a heart shielded by the armour of rancor, and objects, rebounding from it, are cruelly driven away. For centuries we have been involved in an incessant and progressive collapse of values."[14]

This ambivalence was later to have existential import. Ortega was to be one of the expatriated exiles of the Spanish Civil War. But also like Quixote, he sought within the deserts of Spain, an ideal, a new Spain.

> "The author who is writing [this] and those to whom [it] is addressed has its spiritual origin in the denial of a decrepit Spain. But denial by itself is impious. When the pious and honest man denies something, he assumes the obligation to set up a new proposition . . . Having denied one Spain, honor bids us find another. . . . Therefore, if we were observed in our most intimate and personal meditations, we should be found trying out experiments on a new Spain with the humblest fibers of our soul."[15]

It is from this beginning that our intellectual picador fashions his own version of phenomenology, a phenomenology which is "existential" and which focuses upon the circumstances of history and culture.

Ortega and Phenomenology

Historically, Ortega's Germanophilia had already been operational as early as 1904 to 1911, with trips to Germany and studies with the leading neo-Kantians. By 1913, however, Husserl and phenomenology begin to appear in Ortega's thought. Note, however, it is primarily the Husserl of the *Ideas* rather than Heidegger's Husserl of the *Logical Investigations*, which impresses Ortega. The *Ideas* are more "idealist" in contrast to the "realism" of the *Investigations* and of *Being and Time*. In 1913 Ortega wrote several pieces which sympathetically analyse Husserl and phenomenology, and in 1914 Ortega taught a course on Husserl and phenomenology at Madrid. What, in phenomenology, did Ortega adopt?

I begin with a general impression—on reading and rereading Ortega this year, I was much more impressed by the Husserlian ideas which lie behind the surface, than of any Heideggerian influence even though what Ortega got *from* phenomenologists, to my mind, came more from Husserl (and later even more strongly from Scheler and Dilthey) than from Heidegger. Ortega's 1929 *What is Philosophy?* lectures are virtual replicas of a Husserlian styled *Cartesian Meditations* which were given only a bit earlier in Husserl's Paris lectures. To be sure, there are specific Heidegger references in *What is Philosophy?*, the early praiseworthy ones, and the immediate impact of *Being and Time* is noted with some specific echoes, but the core is more Husserlian.

Ortega begins where most phenomenology begins, with *a perceptual based model* of knowledge and with *intentionality*. The combination of these leading ideas leads Ortega into his *perspectivism* which his interpreters note.[16]

The perceptual model with which phenomenology begins, it is now well known, is a gestalt rather than an empiricist one. By gestalt I mean that the basic "simple" for phenomenology is a whole/part relation, or better put, a figure/ground relation. Such a model contrasts with the empiricist sense-atom constructivist notion. Ortega is replete with references and illustrations which follow the phenomenological model. One of the best examples is from *What is Philosophy?*:

> Apparently there was in our perception, along with the immediate presence of the room's interior which we see, a background, though vague and latent, and if this were lacking we would miss it. That is to say, even in the simple act of perception this room was not a thing complete, but only a foreground standing against a vaguely noted background on which we counted, a background that though hidden and somehow attached did exist for us, enfolding what we in fact see. That vague, enfolding background is not now present, but is compresent.[17]

Here, in 1929, prior to Merleau-Ponty, but derived from Husserl, we have the gestalt model of focused present object, located in a contextual field, and situated in a compresent horizon. Ortega's 1913 publications, "Sensation, Construction, and Intuition," and "On the Concept of Sensation" also clearly show a familiarity with and acceptance of Husserl's major critique of empiricist models and the substitution of a perspectival, gestalt model of perception.

Moreover, Ortega's interpretation of perception is early critical of the more essentialist interpretation given it by Husserl and closer to the later existentialized version of perception found in Merleau-Ponty. Note the critique of ideality in perception in the *Leibniz* book:

> If I abstract from this paper everything but its whiteness, this automatically ceases to be the whiteness of *this* paper, and hence *this* whiteness. . . . One does not see what there could be in the intentional act with which I *fix* the whiteness, relating myself to it, which is capable of individualizing that whiteness. Husserl falls into the same complication as the Scholastics for whom . . . the 'species' when it lost its individuality . . . had to take on the new character of generality . . . .[18]

The same sources indicate an acceptance of *intentionality* as a focused, referential activity which reflexively implies a bodily location from which the gestalt is perceived. Again, *What is Philosophy?* makes the correlation of I and world most dramatically clear (and also reveals Ortega's "existential" interpretation of intentionality):

> I am linked with the world—together we are the world and I. And generalizing, we say: the world is not a reality subsisting in itself and independent of me—it is what it is *for* me, and for the moment it is nothing more.[19]

And, again, in Ortega's version of the *Cartesian Meditations*:

> We need, then, to correct philosophy's point of departure. The basic datum of the Universe is not simply that either thought exists, ipso facto, I who think and the world about which I think also exist; the one exists with the other, having no possible separation between them. I am not a substantial being nor is the world, but we both are in active correlation.[20]

There could hardly be a more Husserlian statement. The Ortegean paraphrase of Husserl's ego-cogito-cogitatum correlation is eloquent and places him at the center of a phenomenological perspective. The formal ontology of an intentional correlation is well known in phenomenological scholarship.

And so is the "existentialization" of that formula by Heidegger. In *Being and Time* ego-cogito-cogitatum becomes (Dasein) *being-in-the-World*. Here the functional isomorphism with Husserl should be noted in passing: ego in Husserl becomes the existential Dasein in Heidegger; intentionality as correlation becomes being-in; and the world of cogitata becomes the World. The Heideggerian transformation is one which begins in a critique of the implicit "subjectivism" of Husserl's model of pure consciousness and the substitution of the existent Dasein situated in the World. *Being and Time*, appeared in 1927, but in a similar trajectory, Ortega had begun his similar transformation earlier.

I have already alluded to Ortega's existentialization of Husserl in his 1913 *Meditations on Quixote*. In Ortega, ego-cogito-cogitatum becomes *Man-living (vivencia)-his Circumstances*. The model is both phenomenological and existential. It is phenomenological both in the previously noted sense that circumstances are the field-gestalt notion applied to an immediate and historically experienced world, and in correlation with situated human being. Circumstances are also existential in that they are the concrete circumstances of the surrounding world.

> Circumstance! Circum-stantia! That is, the mute things which are all around us. Very close to us they raise their silent faces with an expression of humility and eagerness as if they needed our acceptance of their offering . . . . We walk blindly among them, our gaze fixed on remote enterprises . . . We must try to find for our circumstance, such as it is, and precisely in its very limitation and peculiarity, its appropriate place in the immense perspective of the world.[21]

Similarly, the correlation between human and circumstances, gets interpreted existentially. In the same year Ortega indicates that his translation of *Erlebnis* is *vivencia*, a term much closer to the sense of being-in-the-world than the observationalist sense suggested by Husserl.

> This word, 'Erlebnis,' was introduced, I believe, by Dilthey. After musing on it for many years in the hope of finding an

existing word in our language to translate it, I have had to give up and turn to neologism. Here is how it was arrived at: in expressions like 'living life,' 'living events', the verb, 'to live' assumes a curious meaning. Without losing its deponent value it takes on a transitive form signaling the kind of immediate relationship into which the subject can enter with certain objects. Now then: what shall we call each instance of this relationship? I can find no other word but 'vivencia.' Everything that arrives at my 'I' with enough presence to become a part of it, is a 'vivencia.'[22]

To experience circumstances, is to *live* them. And to live them, already in *Quixote* is to be immersed in the life of the Spanish historical-cultural context. Thus Ortega's meditations are not upon bare perceptual objects, but upon pleasant experience, the inner ideals of Spanish life, the figures of heroes and maidens, and the like. All very "existential."

This existentialization of phenomenology did occur early with Ortega. This is independent of whether or not his claim that his re-interpretation arose with his criticisms of the Husserlian idea of consciousness which Ortega claims as early as 1914, but which did not get fully explicated until the *Leibniz* book (1947). One can rightly be suspicious of Ortegean "timidity," and of the dating of his most severe criticisms which as we have already seen, tend to become more acute on later occasions. Nevertheless, it is worth noting what he claimed to see lacking in Husserl:

> Since 1914 the basis of all my thinking has been contemplation of the phenomenon of 'human life.' At that time I formulated it—in order to explain Husserl's phenomenology during various courses of lectures—in particular correcting the description of the phenomenon 'consciousness of _____' which, as is well known, at the time constituted the basis of his doctrine.[23]

Although from the same 1947 footnote—I suspect the full critique arose later in time than 1914-he says:

> The description which fits the phenomenon closely—I said then—will state that in a phenomenon of consciousness like perception we find the *coexistence of the I and the thing*, hence that this is not a matter of ideas or intentions but reality itself. So

that in 'fact' perception is what there is: I, on the one hand, being the thing perceived and on the other, being myself; or, what is the same thing, *that there is no such phenomenon as* 'consciousness of _____' as a general state of mind. The reality of my surroundings, and that the presumed description of the phenomenon 'consciousness' resolves itself into a description of the phenomenon 'real human life', which is the *same thing* as the coexistence of the I with surrounding things or circumstances.[24]

In summary: (a) Ortega clearly adapts a basically phenomenological model of interpretation, utilizing the field-gestalt model of perception in correlation with intentionality which pairs I and World; (b) he early existentializes this model by interpreting it not as "consciousness of _____" but as Human-living (vivencia)-Circumstances; and (c) he performs this turn as early as 1913, thereby preceding Heidegger. Thus Ortega does invent a kind of existential phenomenology, but before moving to what he does with it positively, it may be instructive to see what he does *not* do with phenomenology.

Absent is a use of, and I think any deep insight into, *the phenomenological reductions.* Instead there is an early and existential critique of the reductions and reflective consciousness. It is from this critique that Ortega's own version of human existence arises.

Secondly, and much more telling to my point of view, is a virtual total absence of discussion of or use of *variational method.* Variational method is the "motor" which drives the activity of phenomenological analysis and will be, I believe, the essential component which remains relevant to the contemporary situation. It is by means of variational method that phenomenology deals with structure or invariants.

Neither of these elements of phenomenology seem present in use in Ortega. This implies that insofar as Ortega *does* phenomenology, he does it in the mode of the "natural attitude." He is not alone in this practice, but it has specific consequences for Ortega's philosophy. The most obvious such consequence is fairly obvious, I believe, when one compares Ortega's existential phenomenology with that of Heidegger. In Heidegger a structural architectonic is clear and even categorical in *Being and Time.* There are ontological structures to human existence (existentilia, etc.) which are established through phenomenology. These are either absent in Ortega, or at most implicit and latent except in one area. The reason for this contrast lies in both the Ortegean style (philosophy is to result from a more literary approach) and from his only partial adaptation of phenomenology.

Ortega and Quixote

The use of an I-World correlation, common to all phenomenology and distinctively interpreted by Ortega, does remain constant. But in his distinctive existentialization which rejects the "observer consciousness" of Husserl and substitutes "life" and "reality" there occurs a move essentially different from Heidegger. I venture a hypothesis: Whereas Ortega seems to have thought that the Husserlian "observer consciousness," most notorious in the *transcendental ego*, is a result of the reflexive method itself—and thereby Ortega rejects both Husserl's interpretation of the ego *and* the method which constitutes it—Heidegger saw that the interpretation could be rejected without rejecting the new method which constituted it. The results separate the Ortegean and the Heideggerian interpretations of existence.

When we turn to Ortega's partial phenomenological analysis, we note that not only does he reject the reductions and not use variational method, but he also does not follow the order of the reflexive method which always begins with the object correlate or noematic field (the *Cartesian Meditations* first establish world as present rather than existent, then reflexively move back to the ego; *Being and Time* first establishes the worldhood of the World before moving reflexively to Dasein. In this Husserl and Heidegger remain functionally isomorphic). Ortega, it seems to me, simply reinterprets the phenomenological correlation and the result seems therefore much closer to a "phenomenology in the natural attitude." I shall look briefly at this set of movements.

Put off by the Husserlian interpretation of the ego as a kind of observer consciousness, Ortega simultaneously rejects the Husserlian interpretation of the ego *and the means by which it was presumably established*, i.e., the reductions:

Pure consciousness is an 'I' that is aware of everything else. . . .
This 'I' does not *want*, it is only *aware* of wanting; it does not

feel, but only *sees* its feeling. . . . This 'I' is, then, a pure and impassive mirror; it is contemplative and nothing more. What it contemplates is not reality, but only a spectacle . . . '*Bewusstsein von*' makes a ghost of the world . . .[25]

Coupled to the rejection of this interpretation of the ego, is Ortega's simultaneous rejection of the reductions which constitute it. Obviously, what is left out of Husserl's reflexive ego are all the other existential functions: wanting, feeling, acting, etc., a criticism later developed by virtually all existential phenomenologists. But Ortega lays this interpretation of the ego to the door of the phenomenological reductions themselves.

What Ortega does is to immediately substitute an existentialized version of the ego for the Husserlain ego, the ego as *operant, arbiter, executant*.

. . . To suspend what I have called the operative quality of consciousness, its quality as arbiter, is to eliminate what is most basic to it and hence in all *consciousness*.[26]

Such an ego is both active and primary, but in some strange sense, it is also *not*, strictly speaking, "consciousness" according to Ortega.

. . . while an act of 'primary consciousness' is taking place it is unaware of itself, it does not exist for itself. This means that his 'primary consciousness' is not, in fact, consciousness. This concept is an incorrect name for what there is when I purely and simply live, . . . without subsequent reflection. What exists then is myself and the things of various sorts around me.[27]

[What] . . . we find is the *coexistence of I and the thing* Ortega claims, that is what there is and then concludes, that there is no such thing as "consciousness of _____."[28]

What Ortega does, then, is simply to substitute his version of ego for Husserl's, directly as a kind of assertion. What he does not do is either show how this is justified nor give an account of how he reaches this conclusion. Critically, he claims:

> By suspending the executant powers of 'consciousness'. . . .
> phenomenology destroys its fundamental character. 'Con-
> sciousness' is precisely what cannot be suspended; it is
> irrevocable. This is why it is reality and *not* consciousness. . . [29]

Frankly, I do not see that Husserl would have disagreed in this
conclusion, rightly understood, but by renaming "consciousness" reality, Ortega goes on to say:

> The term 'consciousness' ought to be discarded. It was meant
> to stand for the positive, the given, . . . but it has turned out
> to mean just the opposite: it is merely a hypothesis . . . What
> there truly and authentically *is* is not 'consciousness' and in it
> 'ideas' . . . but rather a man existing in a landscape of things,
> in a set of circumstances that also exists.[30]

Whether this is equivalent to returning to the natural attitude
or not, it clearly differs from Heidegger who establishes
Dasein as feeling, wanting, deciding—not directly—but by a
reflexive analysis of how World is presented. Here, then, is an
essential difference between how Heidegger and Ortega differ.
They remain similar only in a surface way in that Heidegger's
Dasein and Ortega's human life are beings who share a set of
similar existential qualities. This is not to invalidate Ortega's
conclusions, it is, however, to wonder how he arrived at them,
from what perspective he "decided" them.

Whatever the executant ego is, there is no doubt in Ortega
that it has its being-in our lives in correlation with a context,
its circumstances. Circumstances are the Ortegean equivalent
to World. And, when we switch to the development of
circumstances, we do find some structural aspects, although
rarely systematically developed.

First, it is clear that circumstances are primarily historicocultural. But they are also multi-layered. At ground level they
are *particular*. And they function as the opening, the perspective
from which wider and more atmospheric considerations can
enter. Here Ortega is, to my mind, clearest and most
self-aware.

Ortega repeatedly affirms that his ground-zero is his
immersion in Spain. Not only does he "[write] my books for
Spaniards, not for humanity,"[31] and acknowledge that his
opening to the very universe is the mountain passes of the

Guadarrama, but his vocation of saving himself only by trying to save his circumstances, i.e., Spanish culture and history, taken up through his journalism, newspapers and constant role as cultural mandarin evidences the seriousness with which he takes the ground level of circumstance. It is also evidence of the *philosophe engagée* of an existential perspective.

If circumstance at ground level perspective is particular, it also becomes a universal at atmospheric levels. Circumstances are openings to the very Universe.

> "What are *circumstances*? Are they only these hundred people? these fifty minutes, this little question? Every circumstance is enclosed by a broader one. Why think that I am only surrounded by ten metres of space? What about those beyond these ten? What a serious oversight, what wretched stupidity it is to take into account but a few circumstances when in reality everything surrounds us."[32]

What we have here is a concentric expansion, from the particular concreteness of a position, a perspective, expanding outward to the Universe.

Again, there is a slight echo of a trajectory similar to that of Heidegger. *Being and Time* took *everydayness (Alltäglichkeit)* as the entrance to the ontological structures of Care, etc. and it would seem that the immediacy of Spanish history and culture is Ortega's base. But, again, we must not over-stress the similarity because the differences are even more important. Everydayness is the *ontical* clue to *ontological* structure as converse to obverse, contra the concentric expansion in Ortega.

However, within the broad concept of circumstance, one also finds what I believe to be Ortega's most unique strengths, primarily relating to historico-cultural phenomena and the philosophy of history. I cannot here develop those notions, but I can point to several of these:

A. One suggestive concept developed by Ortega is that of the *generation*. It might be considered to be a kind of temporal, regional concept. In philosophy it is the movement which finds, in a relatively short period, the growth of a dominant attitude which reacts to and generates a different point of view over an immediately precedent past. Ortega, somewhat strangely I think, believes a generation to be approximately fifteen years in time and usually identifies three overlapping generations within a single time.[33] Whether or not this applies to philosophical movements, I think most of us who teach would recognize something like student generations—there was the generation of "flower children," that of the "silent generation," and now of the "business generation" of neoconservatives. But here the time frame is clearly less than fifteen years, illustrated by a comment by one of my graduate students about defense department recruiting, "In my day this kind of thing was clearly not open—we kept them from doing *that*."

B. Ortega also has a theory of cultural interaction in which *autonomy* exchanges with periods of *cross-fertilization*.[34] This phenomenon, again, plays a role in the history of philosophy, with the autonomous arrival of Greek philosophy and its subsequent European cross-fertilization the dominant phenomenon of the history of philosophy. "There is one exceptional, tremendous, almost monstrous, case, obvious to anyone with a modicum of historical sensibility. I refer of course to the fact that European culture has always been a symbiosis of two cultures: its own and Greco-Roman culture."[35] But this hybrid also has its own heterogeneity:

Greece is probably the most important secret of European history; that is, of the nations that spring up from the ruins of Rome. It is a glorious secret or a crippling one? This is the important question . . . . we ought to ask ourselves whether European culture, so curiously dual in nature, . . . is an integrated, healthy organism or a historical monster, a case of rampant parasitical growth. And if the second, which is the parasite and which the host plant.[36]

This passage, written in 1934, might well find echo in 1983 in philosophy's latest debates about whether or not to abandon and reject "foundationalism" for "edifying" kinds of activities.

C. A third set of historicocultural concepts operational in Ortega's work relates to the dynamic of the history of philosophy, a history forever dying and being born (and in which I find Ortega's best work). It is a history of *surpassed perspectives*.

Not one 'philosophical system' among those formulated appears adequately true to us. Anyone who presumes to be able to settle into some bygone doctrine—and I refer, of course, only to someone fully conscious of what he is doing—is suffering an optical illusion. . . . Unable to find lodging among the philosophies of the past, we have no choice but to attempt to construct one of our own.[37]

What Ortega does in his historical works, is to construct and reconstruct the perspectives from which a philosophy works and pictures its results, but as circumstances change, so do the perspectives. His aim is to avoid both utopianism and skepticism. "At all times and in all places numerous men have existed who 'did not believe in anything,' precisely because 'they did not question anything . . . .' "[38] In short, philosophy's task is the eternal one of critical questioning, deconstructing and reconstructing with respect to circumstances.

What we have in Ortega's philosophy of history, is a kind of *historical* perspectivism.

Indeed, were we to try to summarize this view, the best place to find it stated is by Ortega himself in his essay, "The Historical Significance of the Theory of Einstein." What Ortega claims for Einstein is, in fact, what Ortega himself sought. It is also what places Ortega amidst the contemporaries in philosophical taste. Here is how the essay situates Einstein, the figure who symbolizes Ortega:

1. Einstein rejects the old absolutism of Newtonian absolute space and time and substitutes a relativism of the concrete. Space and Time are embodied, not empty containers. This is what Ortega has done with respect to the ancient philosophies in his existential turn.
2. Einstein's standpoint for his scientific revolution is his *perspectivism*. By decentering the earth, the possibil-

ities of perspectives are freed and so, with Ortega, perspectivism becomes the stance for philosophy.

3. The import of the Einsteinian revolution is the rejection of utopianism and of classical rationalism. So, with Ortega, the implicit totalitarianism of reified utopias and rationalisms are rejected.

4. Finally, Ortega interprets Einstein as a *finitist*, and whether or not this is correct, it is in keeping with the notions of perspective, living (and mortal) being, and the contemporary contrast with classical absolutism. But whereas this is a logical conclusion commensurate with the previous values, here Ortega demurs, and unlike Heidegger whose being-toward-death is an affirmation of finitism, Ortega contends that this conclusion leads to a truncated universe. "Our case is the inverse: the limit signifies an amputation for us, and the closed and finite world in which we are now to draw breath will be, irremediable, a truncated universe."[39]

In this rejection, out of keeping with the other aspects of the contemporary contextualism of Ortega there lies the secret of that strange but highly circumstantial trait: Ortega's *quixotism*. It is with this trait that I conclude and return to the metaphor of the bullfight.

Quixote, in Cervantes' novel, lives in an era which no longer accommodates the holy search he wishes to undertake. So, Quixote in effect, turns the phenomena of his time into the necessary items in his search. A windmill becomes a giant, etc., so that the romantic quest can go on. Something like this lies deeply in Ortega as well, perhaps it is an essential part of the very ground floor perspective from which he views the universe, his circumstance. But it is there.

I have alluded to it in his critical rejection of a deteriorating Spain and his search for a new Spain. But it is even more evident in his romanticism and courtly ideal which comes forth in his ideas about women. Like Quixote, the problem is a relationship between a reified *ideal* and the concreteness of existence. Its least appearance is evidenced in his "Esthetics on a Streetcar," an essay which retells an experience of woman-watching on a short streetcar ride. He begins, "To ask a

Spaniard who has just entered a streetcar not to direct his specialist's gaze over all the women travellers is to ask the impossible."[40] He then goes on to compare the traits observed with esthetic ideals. What is interesting in this early (1916) essay is the critique of the habitual platonistic and quixotic ideal which guides the circumstantial esthetic of woman watching. His description of what he calls a "calculus of feminine beauty" is quite acute. "Today I have taken the streetcar and since I hold that nothing Spanish is foreign to me I have activated that specialist's gaze . . . I have tried to hold in check its insistence, petulance and tactility, and have been very surprised to discover that it has taken less than three seconds to esthetically 'place' the eight or nine women riding on this conveyance and to pass firm judgment of each of them."[41]

Ortega recognizes, in the subsequent discussion of forms of beauty by which the judgment has occurred, that the practice arises out of the Greek side of European and Spanish culture. "Such a theory is a construction, a typical invention of that brilliant Hellenic longing for unity . . . But all this, I repeat, is a construction. There is no single and general model that real things imitate."[42] And while critical, even partially negative to this idealization, Ortega at least concludes that we should judge things for themselves while recognizing that we will also judge them by some distance between themselves and an ideal. He individualizes the ideal, but he does not abolish it. "Therefore, let us measure people in terms of themselves: what each is in reality against what he potentially is."[43] This is even put in quasi-Husserlian language (Husserl, too, is plagued by ideality): "Yes, every book [or woman] is first an intention and then a realization. By the former we measure the latter. The work itself gives us both its norm and its distance from the norm."[44]

But, later, 1929, Ortega seems to return to the two thousand year tradition of a latent ideal which is activated in his description of a woman's side of a love affair.

> In the slumbering depth of the feminine soul, woman, when truly a woman, is always the sleeping beauty, waiting amid life's forest to be awakened by the kiss of the prince. In the depth of her soul she bears, unknowing, the pre-formed image of a man—not an individual man, but a generic type of

masculine perfection. And, always asleep, she moves like a sleepwalker among the men she meets, contrasting their physical and moral figures with that of her pre-existent and preferred model.[45]

Needless to say, such a description is not that of a Gloria Steinem or T. Grace Atkinson! But it is the feminine counterpart of the woman watcher on the streetcar. This inner, ideal—courtly ideal—at the right moment activates the love affair.

> This explains two events which occur in every authentic love affair. One is the suddenness of falling in love: the woman . . . finds herself, suddenly, without process or transition, aflame with love. This would be inexplicable if the casual contact with this particular man had not been preceded by a secret and tacit surrender of her being to that model of a man which she has always carried within herself. The other fact is the way in which the woman, on finding herself deeply in love, not only feels that her love will be eternal . . . but seems to herself to have loved this man forever . . . [46]

This is the expression of the internal ideal by which a human measures himself or herself between potential and actual.

Does this sound strangely archaic to the contemporary ear? (Or, are we at a turning, where history again repeats itself?) If the first, Ortega places himself as a philosophical Quixote, living the two thousand year tradition, if the latter, we reach a Nietzschean revolution of the times.

In the earlier essay concerning the streetcar, Ortega pronounces the inner ideal a construction, in the later a reality. Between the two he vascillates. A similar situation finally closes our circle and returns us to the play of tauromachy. In his late (1946) essay on "The Idea of Theatre," Ortega counterposes the actor and the torero.

First, Ortega distances theatre with reality. In a passage describing a situation in Quixote where, Quixote watching a puppet theatre becomes so involved that he leaves his seat and enters the fray. Ortega contrasts the phantasm of theatre with the reality of action, phantasm collapses when Quixote acts, when "he takes it for reality."[47] Here is the executant ego making a reality in his circumstances.

Then, in the same essay, he makes the curious claim that

unlike the theatre, the circus and the bullring are *not* phantasms—they are real.[48] And he tells of an event in which the most famous actor in Spain, one Isidoro Maiquez, comes to see the most famous torero, Curro Cuchares, in a bullfight.

> Cuchares was having an extremely difficult time killing his bull and the actor, from the front row, was shouting insults and abuse at him. Finally, at one point, when Cuchares found himself facing the bull not far from the section where the actor sat, the bullfighter shouted: 'Miquez, down here dying is no fake the way it is in the theatre.'[49]

But the actor should have responded, "True, one seldom dies in the theatre, but Senor, you should know it is you who have made the bullfight reality, through your executant ego, by taking it for reality." In both theatre and the bullring, Ortega's enigmatic pronouncement holds:

Man is not a *res cogitans*, but a *res dramatica*.[50] And I think I have shown that this is certainly the case for Ortega y Gasset.

Chapter 8

Variation and Boundary: A Conflict within Ricoeur's Phenomenology

Introduction

Paul Ricoeur occupies a unique position among living philosophers in the phenomenological tradition. His work, essentially interdisciplinary, has always been characterized by its dialectic with other points of view. Moreover, his work is such that it is open to those of variant traditions in ways not so clearly the case with his philosophical peers. The year 1983 marked his seventieth year and so the time is ripe for some retrospective evaluation of his itinerary. What I wish to undertake here is an examination of a certain strategy in his earlier work and contrast it with what I take to be a detour into the "anti-phenomenologies" of the post-Hegelian variety, before returning to Ricoeur's more recent work which strikes me again as closer to the trajectory of phenomenology.

In this context, when I speak of phenomenology, I shall do so with regard to what may be called "post-Husserlian" phenomenology. That is, a phenomenology both existential and hermeneutic, a phenomenology which derives from Husserl, Merleau-Ponty and Heidegger. In doing so, I am only too aware of the itinerary Ricoeur has himself taken. It is an itinerary which first claimed to follow more closely the Husserlian program of eidetics than other post-Husserlians took. It is an itinerary which rejects a direct conversion of phenomenology into ontology—Ricoeur's critique of Heidegger—and prefers a method of approximations. And it is an itinerary which draws less explicitly upon the perceptualism of Merleau-Ponty than the dialectics of language via the great detours into Freud, Hegel, the structuralists and analytic philosophy. But it cannot be denied that Ricoeur's version of the tradition is also existential and hermeneutic. He, too, is a post-Husserlian and, if anything, also postmodern in his rejection of the transcendental traditions of the transparent self. But at the same time, his trajectory is one which displays some of the same features which give rise to the tension between the normative and what I shall now call the *openness of the possible*. It is a conflict between *variation* and *boundary* as well as between *description* and the *normative*.

First, however, I must locate the source of the tension, by looking at its methodological location. In phenomenology there is not so much a "Copernican Revolution" as an "Einsteinian Revolution." And this particularly with respect to its basic foundations [—we must be beyond Kant in our metaphors—]. I can say this for the following reasons: The Newtonian conception of space and time and material reality could be said to be one in which an absolute space and an absolute time could be taken as "containers" into which the configuration and motions of matter must fit. The Einsteinian revolution reverses this conception and can be said to, in a sense, generate space-time out of the interplay of concrete complexes of matter. It is simultaneously a correlationalist, a gestaltist and contextualist model for physical reality.

The analogue in phenomenology is not too hard to find. In perception it is the clear and definite shift from an empiricist sense-atom constructionism to a gestalt figure/ground relation. Here the minimum unit is not the abstract quality, or set of them, which could be built up into entities, but is the interplay of multiple figure/grounds with all the variations which become possible upon that interaction.

Similarly, intentionality, rather than being a subject-object division, becomes an interaction between subject and world (the big field upon which all figures can be) in which interaction itself is the variable and yet persistent relation. In Husserl it is intentionality in which the phenomenologically present world is inextricably intertwined with the knowing ego; in Heidegger it is the worldhood of the world which is multidimensionally linked to the being-in of Dasein. And in

Merleau-Ponty it is the interpretation of the world in an intertwining of interrogator-interrogated.

What this Einsteinian contextual and gestalt model means is that every particularity takes its shape and position with respect to its relation and location within a field which situates it.

To make this process clear and simple, I shall take a brief introductory detour into what may be called a model for this "Einsteinian Revolution." And while the use of an illustrative model is not necessarily itself phenomenological, it is in this context very Ricourean in that it will serve as the guiding metaphor for what happens next.

The model will serve to illustrate the relations between variation/boundary and description/normativity which lie behind the problem of Ricoeur's struggle with moral philosophy and literature. (The illustration comes from my *Experimental Phenomenology* [Putnam's, 1977] and in keeping with the phenomenological trajectory, it is a perceptual one.)

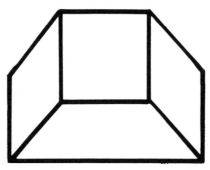

This abstract figure is one of many so-called "ambiguous drawings," or, as I prefer to call them for important reasons, *multi-stable* figures. First, allow a few very quick sets of general observations along the lines already suggested. Whatever this figure is, it is located within and relative to its situating field, i.e., it is a black line drawing on a white, undistinguished field. Although this is obvious enough, it should be noted in passing that strictly speaking the adaptation of such a gestalt model forbids the reductive abstraction of speaking of a thing-in-itself. The thing is what it is *in relation to* and *situated within* its field or context. This point has some importance later on, but even at the historical beginnings of phenomenology this point was not yet totally grasped.

Husserl's movement from a sense-atom constructionism, inherited from the traditions of Modern philosophy, was a gradual one toward the gestalt model ultimately more thoroughly developed by Merleau-Ponty. Thus in his early writings one still finds vestigial references to "sensations," to such strange entities as "hyle," and even references to such non-perceptual entities as "pure tones," and the like. The post-Husserlian tradition is almost unanimous in rejecting this vestigial classical empiricism. I mention this because Ricoeur in his itinerary goes through a similar set of stages in his development of hermeneutics.

Now, however, let us turn directly to the multi-stability of the figure before us. And to make the illustration most appropriate for the examination of Ricoeur's thought, I shall deliberately employ a *hermeneutic device* to elaborate its variations. Ideally, this figure *could* be seen simply as one thing—let us for the moment call it a "hallway variation." In this context the central configuration is seen as "distant" or with its three-dimensional projection to the rear. Now, since in this "Einsteinian Revolution" we must take account of not only the object or *noematic correlate* if we use Husserlian language, but of the position of the observer and the act of seeing, the *noetic correlate*, I shall equally suppose that our observer is a human who lives amidst buildings and other actual material objects which are "like" this drawing. In short, our observer is a "hallway dweller." Now, we can note reflectively a couple of important aspects of this seeing. First, he genuinely can fulfill the reference of his gaze, i.e., see the drawing as a "hallway variation." It is thus a *fulfilled intuition* in Husserl's terms. And it is *apodictic* in that his intuition is genuinely so constituted and is repeatable.

But now imagine that someone from another culture or social-historical group comes along and sees the configuration quite differently—this time as a "pyramid variation." In this case what was the rearward facing central part of the figure is now seen as a forward projection. This can be seen by noting that the apparent position of the observer also changes. Whereas the hallway-viewer is located, as it were, downward from the hall, the pyramid-viewer is almost as it were elevated and viewing the pyramid from above. The thing seen is always correlated in our Einsteinian framework with the position from which it is seen. And, in the hermeneutic context, the common and sedimented experience of the pyramid viewer is also the experiential background within which the figure as pyramid is "natural" and apodictically fulfilled.

Now, take one short step more and we will arrive at where you are all already. Imagine a cross-cultural interchange between hallway-viewers and pyramid-viewers—with or without wars or theological debates—and it will soon be noted that the figure has at least two *equal* stabilities. It is multistable, although in an alternating or mutually exclusive set of variations. When it is hallway it is not pyramid and vice versa—it is a structured ambiguity or multistability. And, from our descriptively analytic level, we can also now discern that whatever the invariance of the figure may be, it shows itself in *variations* which are relative to contexts.

All of this is very Husserlian—and I shall show—very Ricoeurean. But there is one more step which must be taken with our illustrative model. Both variations have been shown to be genuine, intuitively fulfillable, but variant. Yet apodicticity is, in phenomenology, also related to *adequacy*. To suggest how we are to begin to attain adequacy, I must open the door to the deeper possibilities of *variational theory* (which I believe is one of the philosophical techniques which will last even past post-Husserlian phenomenology).

To suggest this line of development, I return once more to our figure. Suppose, now, that we have a very contemporary viewer of things, a young person whose lifeworld is filled with robots, and he or she sees this figure as a "headless robot variation." This gestalt occurs when you see this central configuration as the robot's body, the bottom line as the ground, the lines on the sides as arms and legs, and the verticals as crutches which help guide the sightless robot—and above the body is where the head would be.

When this variation gestalts, you can note that it now takes its place as a fulfillable intuition, as an alternative to the previous two, etc. But, note, this configuration is now not three-dimensionally projected, but is a two-dimensional variation. Nor was this variation likely expected, but once seen, can be seen as a genuine possibility of the figure. I shall not take my example further, but if you are now now phen-omenologically awakened, you might suspect that we have not exhausted the *essential* as contrasted to the empirical possibilities of the drawing.

In each case, particularly in the hermeneutic context I have deliberately suggested, the figure has multistable possibilities and each of these is in an essential sense related to the interpretative context in which the variation is presented. Each intuition was constituted.

I shall now use this illustration as a model—or metaphor, if you like—to explore some aspects of Ricoeur's meditations upon the existential significance of symbols and myths.

Symbols, Myths and the Gestalt Model

The first systematic exploration of the expression of existential signification in which the tension between description and normativity appears is Ricoeur's *Symbolism of Evil.* This book, which I still think is one of his best, explores the field of symbols and myths lying behind the Western traditions awareness of an explanations of evil.

The strategy which Ricoeur uses for this exploration is not unlike that of the Husserl of the "Origin of Geometry" in which one regressively or archeologically moves from high levels of abstraction to lower levels of simple measuring actions. Or, again, the archeology is also like Heidegger's "destruction of the history of ontology" in which one begins with the abstract formal logic of today and deconstructs down to presentational discourse (Rede) in *Being and Time*. In this case, however, it is a movement from the high level abstractions of philosophical explanation down through the sedimented layers of theology, which are then shown to be dependent upon myth, which is then traced down to what Ricoeur calls the "spontaneous confessions of evil," *symbols*.

He undertakes this archeology as an *eidetics*, specifically recalling the Husserlian procedure—and not unlike the earlier Husserl whom Ricoeur seemed to prefer—he ends up with a tactic which retains some vestigial features of empiricist constructionism. It is this problem that I wish to focus upon in this early cut through Ricoeur's itinerary.

First, however, a brief look at the architectonic of *The Symbolism of Evil*. The overall Western field of myths contains, according to Ricoeur, four main strains of myth. The oldest is probably that of order out of chaos, the Babylonian strain, in which order and subsequently the restraint of evil is established "politically," i.e., through the assertion of order over chaos. Here evil is associated with an essentially ambiguous, chaotic state which is to be overcome by imposed and maintained order: A second strain is to be found in the dualistic myths. Here evil is more clearly differentiated from good, but in the form of a duality between mind or spirit and body or matter. This myth is the ancestor of the philosophical myths and the good is regained by controlling and eventually escaping the captivity of matter.

Third, there are the tragic myths in which the Deity itself determines human fate and often in ways which are evil for mortals. Promethius is the tragic figure, who by his very compassion for the human, suffers a divine fate. And, finally, there are the Biblical myths, the myth of Adam, in which God and the creation are essentially good, but evil occurs by an act of will, of disobediance in the paradisaical Garden.

One ingenious feature of this development is that it results in something like an Aristotelean square of opposition in which the fundamental possibilities are recognized and arranged. (Adamic: God is good/mortals originate evil; Tragic: God is bad/mortals suffer and can choose only whether to do so grandly or pathetically; Dualistically good and evil are distinct realms/mortals have to choose the direction and desire for one over the other; or evil is chaos and order good/mortals must establish and maintain order.) And, as *The Symbolism of Evil* shows so brilliantly, it is in the interplay within the whole field that Western consciousness develops. This development is one in which what anthropologists call a "guilt" culture develops, ultimately a culture in which the degree of self-consciousness, linked to awareness of evil, may see itself blamed and guilty whether or not there be gods.

I shall not trace this part of the architectonic further other than to comment that I think *The Symbolism of Evil* still stands as the most brilliant analysis of this theme to date, but also anticipatorily comment that Western guilt culture is not the only phenomenological possibility. Anthropologists frequently differentiate "guilt" from "shame" cultures, of which the largest contemporary example is China. Here one finds a radically different type of self-consciousness, one not touched by the specific development of *The Symbolism of Evil*, but one which poses a limit possibility for precisely that work.

What I shall focus upon, however, is the role and relation of what Ricoeur calls symbols in contrast to myths. For it is here that I detect the vestigial "empiricism" which has not yet disappeared from Ricoeur's early hermeneutics.

In empiricist theories of perception, recall that the bottom line is reached in atomic simples, sense-atoms (or data) which are qualities like "pure" white, shape, etc. From these atomic simples, more complex entities, such as the middle sized objects we usually traffic with, like chairs and tables, are "constructed." I have already noted and illustrated the primary switch to a figure ground, relational model favored by phenomenology as a model for perceptual theory.

In using this as our index, I think we can see that symbols, in *The Symbolism of Evil*, are somewhere between atomic simples in an empiricist model and figures in a phenomenological model. There is, in short, a kind of indecision about what and where symbols are with respect to myths. First, let us note the vestigial atomic simple role: (1) Symbols are clearly the bottom level expressions from which higher level expressions may be developed. In reverse, the archeology of SE digs down to these primary and spontaneous expressions. (2) They are the most simple—although we shall see a symbol isn't anything like a "pure" simple—of the expressions of the awareness of evil. "It is to the least elaborate, the most inarticulate expressions of the confession of evil that philosophic reasons must listen. Therefore we must proceed regressively and revert from the 'speculative' expressions to the 'spontaneous' ones."[1] (3) They play a privileged role in part because they are presumably closer to the emotions, to a kind of direct awareness of evil. From myth, for example, the move to even lower forms of expression, symbols, is projected. "The stratum of myths, to which we are referred by pseudorational speculation, refers us in its burn back to an experience lying at a lower level than any narration or any gnosis."[2] Or, conversely, "there is the language of *confession*, which in the languages of myth and speculation is raised to the second and third degrees."[3] This is to say that symbols are the first degree—approaching zero degree. (4) For these confessions are closest to the blindness, the sheer prelinguistically experienced sense of evil. "The experience of which the penitent makes confession is a bound experience, still embedded in the matrix of emotion, fear, anguish. It is this emotional note that gives rise to objectification in discourses."[4]

Now, as I have already indicated, Ricoeur never goes all the way and the symbol simples are never more than vestigial with respect to the background empiricist model. This for two fundamental reasons: First, there is no sheer prelinguistic level which is reachable for Ricoeur. Even symbols are already *said*. "The Confession expresses, pushes to the outside, the emotion which without it would be shut up in itself. . . . Language is the light of the emotions. Through confessions the consciousness of fault is brought into the light of speech; through confession man remains speech, even in the experience of his own absurdity, suffering, and anguish."[5] But that symbols are bottom level and privileged expressions remains the case.

But, secondly, symbols are not *pure* but multidimensional. "This experience is complex. Instead of the simple experience that one might expect, the confession of sins reveals several layers of experience".[6] And these layers, it turns out, hold in nugatory form, all that is needed for the subsequent elaboration of myth. The levels are "the cosmic aspect of hierophanies . . . the nocturnal aspect of dream productions . . . and the creativity of the poetic word."[7] Hardly a Lockean simple! This, however, should have been expected from the dominant model. Every object, phenomenologically analyzed, turns out to be multidimensional and both more complex and open than first meets naive experience.

Thus even symbol is already in language and is a *latent* hermeneutic, both as experience and expression. "Indeed, it is itself already a hermeneutics, for *the most primitive and least mythical language is already a symbolic language*."[8] The symbol is this complex nexus of significations. "For these realities to be a symbol is to gather together at one point a mass of significations which, before giving rise to thought, give rise to speech. The symbolic *manifestation* as a *thing* is a matrix of symbolic meanings as words."[9] Yet, as bottom line expressions, the hermeneutic is latent, since Ricoeur also claims, "symbols precede hermeneutics."[10] Ultimately, the symbol *donates*, gives to the myth the wealth of meaning it latently holds.

Now, in the terms I am giving this discussion, the symbol

is like the vestigial sense-atom not in structure, but in function. It is the privileged point from which, the origin upon which subsequent elaboration may occur. The function vestigially recalls both a privileged simple and a constructed totality. The symbol, however, in structure is *not* like a sense-atom in that it is multidimensional and *latently* multistable. This multiple possibility of meaning, Ricoeur locates in *equivocity*. "The feeling involved is not only blind in virtue of being emotional; it is also equivocal, laden with a multiplicity of meanings."[11]

In the archeology itself, then, the task is to find the most simple and most archaic of symbols and images. These, Ricoeur finds in a kind of "realist" or "externalist" set of images. Guilt, one possibility of the experience of evil, refers back to sin in which a quasiexternal or better, relational (between God and man) evil is experienced, which in turn refers back to the base which is "a more archaic conception of fault—the notion of 'defilement' conceived in the guise of a stain or blemish that infects from without."[12] Clearly, if so-called primitive cultures are also examples of archaic symbols, the touch/not-touch systems here represent just such an arrangement of experience.

This "realism" also plays another role to be noted for our purposes. It is the role of *literality* for the experience of evil. In his analysis of symbols, Ricoeur opens the way to what becomes a, if not *the* major trajectory of his philosophical itinerary. Symbol, he contends, already contains a double *intentionality*—or, to anticipate—a metaphorical structure.

> "Every sign aims at something beyond itself and stands for that something; but not every sign is a symbol. We shall say that the symbol conceals in its aim a double intentionality. Take the 'defiled' the 'impure'. This significant expression presents a first or literal intentionality that, like every significant expression, supposes the triumph of the conventional sign over the natural sign. Thus the literal meaning of 'defilement' is 'stain,' but this literal meaning is already a conventional sign; ... But upon this first intentionality there is erected a second intentionality which, through the physically 'unclean', points to a certain situation of man in the sacred which is precisely that of being defiled, impure."[13]

Here is the opening to Ricoeur's long *Hegira* in theory of metaphor.

Returning now to the model of phenomenological description, we can now see that symbol plays vestigially the function of a sense-atom as it would in empiricist strategies, but that in structure it is clearly that of a phenomenological object, multilayered, multisignificant and possibly multistable. But it is precisely here that I locate the first problem which I wish to uncover from *The Symbolism of Evil*. *Only so long as the symbol functions vestigially as a sense-atom can it be privileged*. But what if the bottom line is the more post-Husserlian figure/ground model with its contextual interrelations? In this case, rather than symbol as basic, that which *donates* to myth as privileged to derived, the symbol would be seen as at most interactive with its field and, in a strong sense, one could say the field *donates* to the symbol. Or, put more strongly, the field may also in an even stronger sense, be the condition of establishing whatever stability the symbol shows itself.

This, however, would have radical consequences for the architectonic of *The Symbolism of Evil*. At the least, it would be to call into question the privileged role of symbols and to replace this privilege with a gestalt interaction. In short, myth (as field) and symbol (as figure) *together* constitute the basic phenomenon. But this, in turn, means that I could locate the problematic, not so much by having to locate privileged figures or symbols, but from the very midst of *virtually any discourse*. It also makes my "choice" of privileged symbols or figures arbitrary in some fundamental sense. Why should I choose this stability rather than that? Perhaps I chose it because it is most familiar—it is *my* history which I then in Nietzschean fashion affirm, *amor fati*.

Here we reach one juncture at which variation/boundary and description/normativity makes its appearance. What justification is there in taking the "realist" symbols as most archaic? That there might be some cultural anthropological reason is not without merit in that systems of touch/not-touch or *tabu* are widespread in certain cultures. But there are other symbols or figures which could also be so-taken as primitive. Imagine the experience of internal pain. Here is a possible and clearly frequently occurring experience of evil. But its occurrence is internal and its stabilities multiple. It could be "something" inside me and therefore remain with the externalism of the archaic sense Ricoeur favors—and, indeed, the shaministic tricks which excise objects from the body or exorcise spirits constitute the field in which this stability occurs. But, pain symbols may also be stabilized by fields in a strong guilt-like occurrence. And, to suggest a third stabilization, pain can also be read as a disharmonic in which the very location I have within a field is the pain nexus as in some Eastern modes of thought. In each case the reading of the symbol is correlate with the field which locates it.

Even better, however, is to show the multiple stabilities from *stain*, the privileged symbol in *The Symbolism of Evil*. One type of literal stain, surrounded with symbolic significance in many cultures, is menstrual blood. But here the field-stability roles are very different for men than for women. For men the stability might well be that described in *The Symbolism of Evil*. The stain is external, but if touched (the bottom line is touching/touched as a tactile experience) I incur stain, and as constituted by the mythic field, it probably is experienced as fear of women, etc. But the stability for the woman is different, since "stain" is first internal, originates from, etc. Thus in such cultures it is not surprising that the rituals for men are different from those for women. (Am I being naughty and suggesting that the primacy of the "realism" of stain is disguised male chauvinism???)

What I have suggested at the level of symbolism is that had the vestigial sense-atom model of empiricism been thoroughly replaced by the gestalt model, one would have to affirm that whatever meanings one found in symbols are also relative to myths which locate and situate them. Contrarily, symbols by themselves simply are not to be found. Whenever they occur, they do so already in the midst—in the midst of languages at the very least.

Interestingly, this purer gestalt model is also operative in SE, but at a higher level. Once SE has delineated the four types of myths already mentioned, it ascends to the interaction within a field of myths. Each myth, once in contact with others, enters a dynamics which works in complex and subtle ways. For example, the tendency of the Adamic myth to deteriorate to a kind of moralism is halted by the dynamic enrichment of the tragic myth which can be "read into" even the Adamic story. Tragedy always points to an evil *already there* and in the Garden story the serpent is already there, a potential repository for the intentionality of the tragic theme.

But, equally, at the level of myth dynamics, Ricoeur asserts his choice which is for the primacy of the Adamic myth. Here, again, there is a possibility of a tension between the obvious complex openness of myth dynamics and the boundary of a chosen myth primacy. And although Ricoeur does not put the problem the way I have expressed it, he clearly becomes aware of its threat. The route he takes is one which takes him deeper and deeper into the philosophy of language and the development of a complex hermeneutics.

In a revealing self-interpretation, "From Existentialism to the Philosophy of Language," delivered ten years after SE, Ricoeur indicated that the context for SE was an existential phenomenology, concerned primarily with differentiating finitude and guilt—and one can say, to assert the preference for a guilt interpretation over a finitude interpretation, for this is a primary difference between Ricoeur's and Heidegger's interpretations of human existence. But what happened in SE was also the emergence of a hermeneutic problem indicated at the very bottom level of expression, the symbol. Ricoeur says in this later reflection:

> But I must now say that at the time I was not aware of the real dimension of the hermeneutic problem. Perhaps because I did not want to be drawn into the immensity of this problem, I tried to limit the definition of hermeneutics to the specific problem of the interpretation of symbolic language. . . . I defined symbolism and hermeneutics in terms of each other. On the one hand, a symbolism requires an interpretation because it is based upon a specific semantic structure, the structure of double meaning expression. Reciprocally, there is a hermeneutical problem because there is an indirect language. Therefore I identified hermeneutics with the art of deciphering indirect meanings.[14]

Those who read Ricoeur know how far this development went. There were the detours into Freud and Hegel, the sophistication of a dialectic of a "hermeneutics of suspicion" and a "hermeneutics of belief," and later the therapies of structuralism, linguistic studies and analytic philosophy. So that now Ricoeur can conclude, "Today I should be less inclined to limit hermeneutics to the discovery of hidden meanings in symbolic language and would prefer to link hermeneutics to the more general problem of written language and texts."[15]

Here we have an interesting example of a self-aware transition, a transition from what I shall call a *metaphor hermeneutics* to a broader *text-world hermeneutics*. In what follows, I shall contend that this movement is one which more thoroughly adopts a gestalt model of interpretation and increasingly leaves the vestigial sense atom model. But it is also a movement which occurs through the therapies in particular of the linguistically oriented disciplines of the twentieth century. Ironically, it is also a movement which, while enriching Ricoeur's notion of linguistic phenomenology, was already operational in the perceptualist model of earlier existential phenomenology.

Phenomenology and the Linguistic Therapies

In the self-exposition of "From Existentialism to the Philosophy of Language," Ricoeur claims a shift of emphasis for himself, a shift which effectively occurs between what I have called metaphor hermeneutics and text-world hermeneutics. Metaphor hermeneutics is the hermeneutics marked by a double intentionality, already noted in the analysis of symbols. In the period immediately following SE, Ricoeur significantly sophisticates this bi-level hermeneutic by his detour through the challenges to direct consciousness. The figures of Freud, Marx and Nietzsche introduce a reductive form of metaphor hermeneutics, a hermeneutics of "false consciousness" in which the hidden meanings which are recovered are other than initially thought. It is from this period that Ricoeur develops his well known conflict of a "hermeneutics of suspicion" versus a "hermeneutics of belief" (with the latter heavily indebted to the originator of double hermeneutics, Hegel). Note that in both cases hermeneutics is directed toward a *recovery* of lost meaning or hidden meaning. Only in both cases one can no longer deal with apparent meanings in a "first naivete." Matching the critique of transparent meaning must be the critical stance of "second naivete," which is the intellectual attitude of this sophisticated and critical metaphor-hermeneutics.

There is a sense in which this sophistication of both a two-level and a dialectical suspicion-belief hermeneutics reaches an end, the development of metaphor-hermeneutics. But meanwhile, Ricoeur is also encountering a very different strain of thought, the linguistic disciplines of the twentieth century: structuralism, linguistics and analytic—particularly Ordinary Language—philosophy. And I discern in this encounter what appears to me to be a more significant shift of sensibility, a shift which leads to what I am calling *text-world hermeneutics*.

On the surface this shift is one which lies in the discovery that what had been taken as a special problem with symbols, is in fact a general problem with language. And insofar as the multistability of symbols now gets recognized as a general problem of language, hermeneutics must ascend from the special discipline of the exegesis and interpretation of special (holy) texts, to the general discipline hinted at by Dilthey, Schliermacher and then Heidegger.

But for my purposes here, this gradual shift to a general hermeneutics is also a shift which returns Ricoeur to a much more thoroughly phenomenological model of interpretation, an interpretation which finally adapts in a much more significant way the gestalt model which has been at the core of phenomenological insight.

Thus I shall briefly turn to some of the salient features which emerge in this move to the philosophy of language.

What may be noted immediately is that there is a virtual isomorphic transfer of special problems in SE to general problems in the philosophy of language. Symbols, in SE, potentially take their places in a field of myth and structurally, as noted, they are already multidimensional and multistable. This phenomenon, however, also occurs in the field of language and early on Ricoeur redevelops the interplay between *word* and its fields (sentences, speech contexts, or the system of language). But whereas in SE symbols are in effect "privileged words," in ordinary language *all* words display multiple stabilities within linguistic fields.

Word, then, becomes a kind of focal object or figure which is to be related to its field as the task of a linguistic phenomenology:

1. It is *polysemic*. Its meaning is both multidimensional and multistable. Semiotically, as in the structuralist context, words are merely elements in a system of language. They are

"differences" which are clearly relative to the language context. Here we have an infusion of contextual field. The word changes in relation to its position within language as the focal object changes in relation to its field. (2) It is *multistable*. At the semantic level, in ordinary language, there are a multiplicity of possibilities determined by contexts, the contexts of speech acts. Such contexts are temporal and situated, and therefore open (in contrast to the presumed closedness of the semiotic situation). (3) The word also functions in terms of and always in relation to a larger field. Words are situated in sentences— and words also may function as sentences making the surrounding field a matter of spoken to unspoken. Again, we see re-emerging the basic gestalt model which guides phenomenological insight.

Each of these elements may be found repeatedly in Ricoeur's more recent work. What we may glean from this emergent emphasis is that: (a) What was taken as a special problem of symbols, turns out to be a structural element of language in general. (b) The model of the sense atom, in which complexities are built upon simples, is gradually discarded because the very base itself turns out to be the complexity of *polysemy*. (c) This polysemy, we have noted, is what it is by virtue of its gestalt character. Thus we find Ricoeur's transition from metaphor hermeneutics to *text-world* hermeneutics to a move to precisely the more central model of phenomenology, a phenomenology increasingly freed of its vestigial "empiricism."

What is of interest to me in this transition is precisely that it should have been through the linguistic disciplines that Ricoeur returns—as it were—to phenomenology. How can this be? Part of the answer lies in Ricoeur's persistent habits of thought. He has, to his credit, always taken his counterparts seriously. When he undertakes studies in Freud, he reads the entire opus and, moreover, reads sympathetically and in such a way that he seeks to incorporate the challenge even into his own trajectory. The same applies to each of the detours which have characterized his thought paths.

But this seriousness also has its dangers. And in the cases of the mid-period, the high development of metaphor-hermeneutics, the danger is apparent. Hegel, Freud, Marx and Nietzsche, all with their hermeneutics of double meaning, wherein strategies of reduction or of recovery, remain functionally with a foundationalist metaphysic. Whatever appears—whether to first intentionality, to first naivete, to simple referential meaning—hides a ground which is other, but which explains the "illusion" of appearance. Whether this ground is Spirit, the unconscious, the structures of productivity, or the will-to-power, it functions metaphysically. And metaphysics is the opposite of a rigorous phenomenology. This, not because of the contrast of vestigial direct and transparent consciousness—a language endemic to Husserl but belied by the way in which he actually operated—but because of the way in which phenomenology develops the gestalt model which is discovered through the radical use of variational method.

I would contend that in this very seriousness, at the peak of metaphor metaphysics, Ricoeur is led away from the most positive insights of phenomenology. But he returns to these insights by taking a new set of methodological others—the linguistic disciplines. There is a strange underground liaison between these disciplines and what lies within the central phenomenological model.

I cannot here trace the intricacies of each of these methodological others, but I do wish to at least impressionistically suggest where the liaisons lie. First, with respect to structuralism and the development of a semiotic linguistics: Structuralism constitutes language as a system, a system of relations within which oppositions occur. Now one thing Ricoeur has taught us is to look beyond the explicit claims at theoretical justification, and to focus upon how the discipline functions. In his own first critiques of structuralism, Ricoeur attacked the atemporality of structuralism, its exclusively synchronistic emphasis, and countered it with a temporalistic hermeneutic. But this is not where I see the issue relevant here.

What structuralism did with respect to language, by its very constituting of language as a finite system of differences, was to establish language as a *field*. The parallelism with my perceptualist model is suggestive—the linguistic field, like the visual field within which our objects of vision occur, is the field within which objects (words) occur in a field of possible constructions (sentences). And for our purposes, whatever other effects the structuralist analysis might imply, this re-establishes the primary gestalt feature in which words are what they are only in relation to the field within which they occur. Negatively, and important for the removal of the sense atom model, there can be no privilege to any word or any arrangement within the semiotic system. Such a horizon-talization of values *functions* very much like a phenomenological reduction and opens the linguistic field both to its finitude and its universality. And, through the specific application of variations, one can begin to discern the invariants or structures of that field.

In this interpretation, in spite of its disregard for the subject, for its strange theory of unconsciousness, etc., structuralism opens the way for Ricoeurean hermeneutic to return to phenomenology. The linguistic field may become the "world" of possible significations within which specific *texts-worlds* take their appearance.

And with this shift to a latently gestalt model, we begin to leave sense atom models behind. But what was the motivation for the vestige in the first place? I think the answer lies in Ricoeur's admirable and even dogged insistence upon what I shall call a *realist* (or externalist) function. His worries about phenomenology have always been worries about its possible idealist drift, its subjectivism. Note how this realist emphasis occurred in SE. The symbol is the closest to the lower level where "raw experience" comes in touch with language. And the privileged touch symbol is precisely the one which most approximates externality.

This problem, after the shift to the philosophy of language, is transformed into the general problem of *reference*. Thus beyond the closure of semiotics, is the realism of reference. Beyond the level of semiotics, there is the level of semantics. And in this context the challenging methodology becomes Analytic philosophy, particularly in its Ordinary Language form.

Ricoeur rightly notes the development in the analytic tradition, most clearly in Wittgenstein, which moves from a simple—one might call "first naivete"—theory of reference to the later polysemic theories of reference in late Wittgenstein, Austin and Searle. But what this later—"second naivete"—theory of reference does in effect is to become aware again of phenomenology, a phenomenology which would escape both the futility of mere linguistic distinctions and the unverifiability of all claim to direct intuition of lived experience. Thanks to the grafting of linguistic analysis to phenomenology, the latter may be cured of its illness and find its second wind.[18]

Is this a second wind, or a return to what is basic in phenomenology? In either case, it is, finally, to have left the vestigial constructionism of the sense atom model.

And this move also allows what I have called text-world hermeneutics to emerge more clearly and more precisely in a phenomenological sense. Once more, I wish to make a few brief allusions to the way in which Ricoeur's recent hermeneutic strategies are now more rigorously phenomenological. (1) Ricoeur has for several decades sought to desubjectify phenomenology in two senses. First, the subject cannot be thought of as "first" nor as transparent. Indeed, understanding the subject is arrived at indirectly, by way of its situation in the world. Second, the subject must be understood by moving first from its world—in the linguistic phenomenological sense—from its world of meanings. But this is equivalent to reasserting the essential movements of intentionality and its analysis. Husserl, in the most idealistic *Cartesian Meditations* had first to establish the presence of world as phenomenon (in contrast to its Cartesian "existence") and Heidegger begins the analysis of human existence by establishing the worldhood of the world.

Ricoeur, in text-world hermeneutics, in similar fashion, turns first to the problem of the "world of the text." This is to say, that its *noematic* or object-correlation is what must first be discovered. This move avoids the problem of the author's intentions of mere subjective designs and the like, and looks primarily at what may be called the gestalt configuration of the text world. But this, I contend, is what is uniquely phenomenological in the first place, at least latently in the gestalt model.

2. Secondly, in the move to the philosophy of language, there may now be seen to be a vast multiplicity of texts, of text worlds. And each of these is contexted, situated, often in an analogue with SE, within a wider field of meanings. And so for the second time we move away from simple privilege. There is,

the gestalt character of significance and context. Speech acts, now with intentionality, human action, the social setting of language, become the necessary set of items to be taken into account. Note what Ricoeur has to say about the contribution of Ordinary Language philosophy to this set of problems:

> First, it has proved that ordinary language does not, cannot, and must not function according to the model of ideal languages constructed by logicians and mathematicians. The variability of semantic values, their sensitivity to contexts, the irreducibly polysemic character of lexical terms in ordinary language, these are not provisory defects or diseases which a reformulation of language could eliminate, rather they are the permanent and fruitful conditions of the functioning of ordinary language.[16]

What is this but a simultaneous rejection of sense-atom constructionism and a reassertion of gestalt contextualism? This reaffirmation of phenomenology occurs by way of the detour into ordinary language philosophy.

In Ricoeur's appraisal of ordinary language philosophy, he notes that not only is it sensitive to the nuances of descriptive power in certain areas, but that it has implications for hermeneutics:

> . . . Hermeneutics may draw some benefit from an accurate inquiry into the functioning of ordinary language. I have already alluded to the connection between the functioning of symbolic discourses and the polysemic structure of our ordinary words. We may extend the parallelism further: understanding, in the most ordinary sense of the word—let us say conversation—is already an intersubjective process. . . . to understand discourse is to interpret the actualizations of its polysemic values according to the permissions and suggestions proposed by the context.[17]

And, again, we see a clear shift to a gestalt model which guides phenomenological method, now applied to the field of linguistic performance. In short, through the linguistic disciplines, Ricoeur comes precisely to that point which he calls for:

> Now the recapturing of the intentions of ordinary language experiences may become the major task of a linguistic

in fact, something like an infinity of possible texts and with these we again reach the dilemma of variation and boundary. Both the essential polysemy of words—which Ricoeur now sees as the basic condition for symbolic discourse itself and the actualization of polysemic values provided by contexts—now complicate as well as renew the hermeneutic task.

Conclusion

The implications for this shift are, with respect to Ricoeur's earlier position, negative. But they are also implications which more thoroughly establish Ricoeur as simultaneously phenomenological and at least potentially within the nonfoundationalist modes of philosophizing which are emerging in the twentieth century. If the gestalt model I have suggested does indeed lie at the heart of phenomenology, it becomes clear that such possibilities as hierarchized models of language must also fail. Idealized languages as privileged, privileges to some particular set or type of expressions, or direct derivations of normative or actional recommendations from such phenomena fail.

But, positively, the switch within a now linguistic phenomenology to the non-foundational gestalt model is one which to my mind does return us in a new way to that desire for the real underlying Ricoeur's itinerary. Our world—not unlike the complex, multistable world of texts—is a world of multiple cultures and forms of life. And just as the now more sophisticated text-world hermeneutic finds its task as one of discerning the nexus of invariants amidst the plethora of variations, so does this reflect the essential multistability of life contexts.

Ricoeur's Hegira is a journey which returns us exactly to this point. And in the process he has deepened our understanding of interpretation which in turn has deepened our understanding of the interpreting animal—ourselves. And in most cases it is probably preferable to be deep than merely to be conclusive.

Chapter 9

Epilogue: Response to Rorty, or, Is Phenomenology Edifying?

Response to Rorty

Were philosophers to have Academy Awards, and were reviews in the major journals and such national papers as the *New York Times* or the *New York Review of Books* nominations, then Richard Rorty's *Philosophy and the Mirror of Nature* would certainly have won the 1981 "Oscar." For that book, with only one contender,[1] surely received more attention than any other philosophy book for that year. The interest spread to Stony Brook, too, for in the fall term Patrick Heelan organized an informal seminar of some twenty faculty and doctoral students to read *Mirror*. I was, due to a schedule conflict, unable to attend, but soon began to hear discussion in the hallways.

Bits and pieces began to take shape: "Rorty's decreed the end of analytic philosophy." "Rorty's turning Continental." "Rorty thinks that the three greatest philosophers of the twentieth century are the late Heidegger, the late Wittgenstein, and Dewey." And, most often from my ACE[2] colleagues— "Well, its about time somebody from the establishment discovered what we've known all along about the state of contemporary philosophy." Still, I had not read the book.

Then the reviews appeared, repeating in many ways the above conversation in more academic prose. Some beleived that with Rorty's strong emergent interest in *hermeneutics* evidenced in Mirror and with the repeated references to Heidegger, Habermas, Apel, Derrida, that he had, after all, opened the way to Continental philosophy. Moreover, his scathing critique of what some identified as analytic philosophy was unmistakable.

But it was not until early 1983 that my own schedule allowed me to read the book. (I admit to some grudging reluctance at first, since, from the secondary information, I, too, believed that Rorty was a Johnny-come-lately to a perspective on contemporary philosophy which many of us arrived at fifteen or even twenty years ago! His choices of representative giants had even been anticipated in print far earlier, and again by William Barrett in his 1978 the *Illusion of Technique*. Barrett chose two of the same individuals, although he substituted William Jones for John Dewey, but with much the same impact. Moreover, the death of Modern Philosophy, i.e., the "foundationalism" of the Cartesian sort, had been decried by virtually every "classical" phenomenologist in all three varieties—transcendental, existential, and hermeneutic). Thus when I began to read, I received something of a surprise. First, the bulk of the book did not really have so much to do with anything like either a conversion to Continental philosophy or a deathknell for analytic philosophy that the secondary interpretations seemed to emphasize. Rather, there was a reworking of a total perspective upon contemporary philosophy which in its most penetrating sense did not even distinguish clearly between analytic and Continental forms.

Surely, Rorty's audience remained the AE, and his rhetorical and conceptual style remained clearly within those boundaries. I have already remarked upon the obvious invisibility of those who in ACE were already quite aware of the negative side of *Mirror's* result. *Mirror*, was, in the thrust of its attack, a kind of Kuhnian shift, a change of model or of categories by which one could interpret contemporary philosophy. It was a shift which, negatively, did claim that the end of Modern philosophy, insofar as it was a systematic, epistemological-metaphysical enterprise which constructed itself upon a *foundational* base, was no longer tenable. This was not exactly news to many of us—but what Rorty did further, was to develop the thesis such that his emergent perspective which differentiated between foundational and edifying *hermeneutic* philosophy cut across *both* analytic and Continental fronts. Its result was, on one level, to undercut much of what

had been taken for granted as differences between the two
styles of philosophy, and replace it with another.

I also found that I had to take Rorty at his word
concerning what he was doing, for this attack upon
foundationalism in both analytic and Continental groups,
arose primarily from within analytic philosophy itself, from its
more pragmatist sources. Rorty claims:

> . . . I began to read the work of Wilfred Sellers. Sellers' attack
> on the Myth of the Given seemed to me to render doubtful
> the assumptions behind most of modern philosophy. Still
> later, I began to take Quine's skeptical approach to the
> language-fact distinction seriously, and to try to combine
> Quine's point of view with Sellers'. Since then I have been
> trying to isolate more of the assumptions behind the
> problematic of modern philosophy, in the hope of generalizing
> and extending Sellers' and Quine's criticisms of traditional
> empiricism.[3]

The hard core of *Mirror* is exactly that. From within the larger
analytic movement, Rorty has taken a pragmatist, anti-
foundationalist stance and argued that all forms of analytic
foundationalism are untenable. This is clearly a severe attack,
for it implies that the "science model" held by the early
Positivists and retained through most foundationalistic
philosophy must go.[4] And, if correct in a Kuhnian sense, this
would also mean that a lot of what is taken as "normal"
problems for analytic philosophy would not so much be solved
or reworked, but simply disappear, become "uninteresting."
This would be the case for much of the so-called body-mind
problem as well. Philosophies are, of course, rarely responsive
to refutations. Historically they either tend to be abandoned
rather than die of rebuttal, or, more likely to undergo
resuscitation by revision. Thus analytic foundationalism has in
very recent years, re-emerged as the New Realism Rorty refers
to in his later *Consequences of Pragmatism*.

The internal attack, addressed to analytic philosophers.
clearly arose primarily from Rorty's own readings of that
tradition and its problems. This is clear both in the form and
substance of the attack. Nor does it repeat the same kind of
criticism made much earlier by both Husserl and Heidegger.
Indeed, I suspect Rorty would think of their attacks as still

within the foundationalist framework since it is possible to interpret Husserl as rejecting Cartesianism on behalf of transcendental idealism, and Heidegger's destruction of the history of ontology which covers over a more ancient and favored ontology as yet another foundation.

However, in one crucial way Rorty's attack does function like the earlier attacks of Husserl and Heidegger. Rorty's "paradigm shift," which resituates a perspective upon contemporary philosophy, is in practice something like the deliberate tactic of a "paradigm shift" employed by Husserl well before Kuhn. Husserl made such a shift of perspective an essential and deliberate part of phenomenology itself. This tactic, buried for some beneath his intricate machinery, is nevertheless exactly a purposeful shift of perspective. I refer, of course, to what Husserl called the shift from the "natural attitude" to the "phenomenological attitude," a shift which was both deliberate and fundamental for a different kind of "seeing" to occur. The elaborate steps of the *reductions* which appear in most of Husserl's works are the parts which go together, or better, the set of hermeneutic instructions which tell how to perform the shift. Unfortunately, too many interpreters simply either got lost in the intricacies, or worse, read Husserl literally.[5] What was important was to be able to experience what is seen differently, which, once attained make the instructions either intuitive or unnecessary. (In a sense, Kuhn describes what happens in a shift, but how it happens remains for him, largely unconscious. Husserl attempts to make shifting a deliberate procedure, a phenomenological rationality.)

The common perceptual model between Husserl and Kuhn is the *gestalt shift*.[6] Gestalt shifts, either those which take ambiguous figures and grounds, are mini-illustrations of changes of perspective. Paradigm shifts or the shift from the "natural" to "phenomenological" attitudes are, of course, both more sweeping and more fundamental. But it is clear that Husserl made this phenomenon one central element of his own phenomenology. Rorty, with reference to the field of contemporary philosophies, practices such a shift.

Rorty's shift at its highest level of abstraction, divided contemporary philosophies into those which are *foundational* and those which are non-foundational. Then, within those which are non-foundational, he discerns a certain pattern which he terms alternatively *edifying* or *hermeneutic* This is to say that the negative side of *Mirror*, the attack upon foundationalisms, is matched by a positive side, the development of a generic hermeneutic or edifying philosophy. It is here that the representative giants take their shape and role: late Heidegger, late Wittgenstein, and Dewey.

If each reject systematic, hierarchical, structural and foundational philosophical erections, particularly those of the Modern or Cartesian and Kantian sorts, then what is to be accepted also has need of clarification. For Rorty, language remains the guiding thread. In his preface, he indicates that what unites all he learned from the variety of his teachers and philosophical education was:

> I treated them all as saying the same thing: that a "philosophical problem" was a product of the unconscious adoption of assumptions built into the vocabulary on which the problem was stated—assumptions which were to be questioned before the problem itself was taken seriously.[7]

This remains a central philosophical axiom with Rorty and he has even produced a lexicon translating the main terms of *Being and Time* into vocabulary language.[8]

Language is a twentieth-century obsession for philosophers, both Anglo-American and Euro-American. But what is common to the giants Rorty cites is what may be called a certain *horizontalization* of language. Negatively, this is a rejection of hierarchies to language and specifically a rejection of the language/metalanguage developments of foundationalists. Wittgenstein, in the later "language game" and *Philosophical Investigations* period, of the three giants, was the most explicit about this connection. But the movement in Heidegger from the apparant structural foundationalism of *Being and Time* to the increasing hermeneutic horizontalization in his late work follows the same trajectory.[9] And, Dewey, although not directly concerned with language in the same way, unites both in his deconstruction of the sciences into human problem-solving activities which, again, are horizontalized.

Horizontalization implies negatively that there are no privileged language games, no disciplines, no privileged activities. There are only appropriate or inappropriate contexts and a diversity of fields. What seems as a kind of democratic anarchism here, Rorty seems to apply to the very profession of philosophy. It must take its place as one type of conversation among others. Certainly, philosophers can no longer pretend to be either the overarching thinkers of the past, nor cultural mandarins with a higher authority. They can be *edifying* in the sense of a moral concern:

> The only point on which I would insist is that philosopher's moral concern should be with continuing the conversation of the West, rather than with insisting upon a place for the traditional problems of modern philosophy within that conversation.[10]

This is a modest view of philosophy, an essentially communicative, interpretative one. But Rorty intends it to be positive within this modest position—his choice of edifying is deliberate:

> Since "education" sounds a bit too flat, and *Bildung* a bit too foreign, I shall use "edification" to stand for this project of finding new, better, more interesting, more fruitful ways of speaking.[11]

Moreover, edification is essentially a *hermeneutic* activity which, in its new mode:

> The attempt to edify (ourselves or others) may consist in the hermeneutic activity of making connections between our own culture and some exotic culture or historical period, or between our own discipline and another discipline which seems to pursue incommensurable aims. . . . It may . . . consist in the "poetic" activity of thinking up . . . new aims, new words, or new disciplines, followed by, so to speak, the inverse of hermeneutics: the attempt to reinterpret our familiar surroundings in the unfamiliar terms of our new inventions. In either case, the activity is . . . edifying without being constructive.[12]

One can detect here a certain "Continental" drift but still within Rorty's constant of philosophy as linguistic activity. In the sense and to the extent that Rorty has seriously absorbed the lessons of Continental hermeneutics, the notion that he has turned toward Continental philosophy is only partly true. But insofar as hermeneutics is itself interpreted as linguistic activity, having to do with a kind of Rortean language game in which new vocabularies are made, discovered, or whatever, the hermeneutics takes its place within his overall analytically conceived notion of vocabularies and their unconscious assumptions. In this respect *Mirror* is simultaneously analytic and Continental, while, equally simultaneously, it shifts the divisions of philosophy such that the high level difference between foundational and edifying philosophies cuts across both analytic and Continental philosophies.

Although I must return to the notion of horizontalization which plays such a crucial role in edifying philosophy, it may be of interest to see how the Rortean scheme might divide the field of phenomenological philosophies. (As I noted in the Introduction, Rorty effectively ignores phenomenology as such and in the few instances where it appears at all it is identified, particularly in Husserl, as belonging to the foundational enterprise.) Is all phenomenology foundational? Or are there foundational and edifying phenomenologies?

Is Phenomenology Edifying?

At first reading Husserl would indeed seem to be a prime candidate for a foundational philosopher. The architectonic of his overall work clearly has that structure. He is avowedly a *transcendental* thinker, placing himself in that respect in the Descartes-Kant traditions. He "founds" his architecture upon the ground of transcendental (inter) subjectivity. He claims phenomenology as a "rigorous science," a new science, thus not unlike Positivism, incorporates his version of a science model into his method. Moreover, most of his critics and scholarly interpreters have taken him that way.

Yet there are elements within his philosophy which are implicitly antifoundational. Interestingly, these are the devices of method which make phenomenology function as a *horizontalization* of phenomena. These are sometimes hard to detect because they must be isolated from within the apparent structure or foundationalist architectonic which scaffolds Husserl's edifice.

In this respect, the strategy of Husserl's *Cartesian Meditations* is peculiarly instructive. Husserl simply accepts the structure or framework of Descarte's project, but then, step by step, he replaces each element with a radically different result. For example, on the surface it seems that Husserl's and Descartes' foundations are the same: the *ego cogito*. But in the end, they are not. Descartes' ego is (a) the self-enclosed subject, (b) worldless except by inference or "geometric method," (c) a subject without object, etc. Husserl's transformations replace each of these elements: (a) the (phenomenologically present) world is equiprimordial with and strictly correlated with the ego; (b) the ego, thereby is *not* self-enclosed, and in fact is reached only by way of the world; (c) there is no subject without an object, nor object without a subject. In short, the whole building has been replaced and the scaffolding alone gives the semblance of a Modern philosophy.

Another, more Rortean way of phrasing this is to say that what remains after Husserl's *deconstruction* of Descartes is a new vocabulary. It is the vocabulary of the correlation of noema-noesis, of I and World, of *correlationsapriori*. Moreover, if anything is "given" in Husserl, it is what is always "given" in the Rortean scheme, *some vocabulary*. Then, within this vocabulary, there are grammars of movement about how one may go in one or the other direction. I shall contend below that these hermeneutic rules at the core are the *variational methods* which derive from phenomenology. But in both senses, what remains of the Modern project is scaffolding—the problem is that Husserl was always proud of his scaffolding! This is evidenced by the vast amount of his publications which had to do with describing it in the multiple ways he did (how many reductions are there? how many ways of getting to the ego? to the phenomenological world? etc.).

It has always been my contention—admittedly disputed by many literal-minded Husserlians—that Husserl's method was heuristic. Over and over again, he adopted the terminology and the structures of Modern philosophy in both its Cartesian and Kantian forms, but in each case he reworked elements and structure, such that they no longer meant what they originally did. In his last work, *The Crisis*, he noted that what he called the "phenomenological attitude" was not, as often earlier described, a device of method, but a permanent acquisition of the philosopher. But, as I shall contend below, the result of this shift of perspective—even in Husserl—is one which is fundamentally nonfoundational.

What is hard to decide concerning Husserl himself, is how much of the radicality implied in his work was discerned by him. There is no doubt that he was wedded to his terminology of "transcendental idealism," even if transcendental meant for him something radically different than in the Modern traditions and even if idealism also was intended to be different from all other idealisms. But there is little doubt that the two founders of variant phenomenologies both rejected transcendentalism (and at least by implication, foundationalism) and saw some of the more radical implications of Husserl's methodology.

Merleau-Ponty's existential phenomenology early claimed that the implication of phenomenology was not transcendental, with all the hubris of a total and self-contained system, but existential. Moreover, the late Merleau-Ponty reworks the I-World vocabulary of Husserl into an ongoing set of interrogations as in *The Visible and the Invisible*. No foundational standpoint is possible, but the polymorphy of the intertwining with its open-ended implications replace the Husserlian scaffold entirely. Similarly, Heidegger's *hermeneutic* phenomenology, although retaining a vestigial foundationalism in *Being and Time* moves as Rorty himself has seen and appreciated in a nonfoundational direction. The expositional debate in this case revolves around Heidegger's gradual dropping of phenomenological terminology, the ambiguity as to whether what he *does* remains essentially phenomenological, and whether or not the moves into his later terminology arose through the very implications of the earlier, more explicit phenomenology.[13] Thus, if phenomenology can still be used to characterize its existential and hermeneutic versions, in its later phase it becomes ever more explicitly nonfoundational.

This excursus, however, is historical and interpretive. What is needed here to expose the edifying and nonfoundational aspects of a phenomenology, is to show from its very core what motivates this possibility. Is phenomenology edifying?

To accomplish this move I shall take two seemingly contrary steps. First, I shall try to show that the edifying or hermeneutic thrust of phenomenology can be found in or arise from essentially *Husserlian* notions (while not denying that non-foundationalism becomes more explicit in the post-Husserlians). And, second, I shall focus not just upon the concepts and explicit claims about phenomenology, but upon philosophical *praxis.* What dissolves the apparent contrariness between the "antique" and contemporary situations itself arises from the tradition of philosophical practice. In all of this I admit that not all *scholars* of the tradition would agree with me—but I suspect most practitioners would.

The scaffolding of which Husserl was so proud, here interpreted as a set of hermeneutic rules for proceeding, included an emphasis upon experience and evidence. Experience must be actual or fulfillable; evidence is *intuitive* (that which in fulfillment is present). What most standard interpreters have taken this to mean is that whatever is intuitively *given* provides not only some kind of foundation, but belongs to the myth of the given (and Sellers was one of these interpreters). But this interpretation misses entirely the role of evidence and intuition as hermeneutic rule *to discover something else.*

For even within the heart of Husserl's explicit set of procedures, he follows what, to my mind, was a mistaken heuristic which confuses issues. The surface or explicit steps, when put into *practice,* reveal *not* the above kind of given, but something quite contrary. *For phenomenology, intuitions are constituted, not given.* Only already constituted intuitions are "given" *within an already sedimented context.* When taken as "evidence" the evidence is strictly indexical (thus hermeneutic.) What the scaffolding allows one to get at is the relationality between experience and contexts or fields. All experience is *context-relative.* Here, at a most basic level is a first clue to phenomenological *horizontalization.*

A second "device of method," as scaffolding, is the shift from "natural" to "phenomenological" attitudes. This deliberate shift, however, is not a shift on similar levels. The phenomenological attitude is *the access to context relativity.* That is why it must become permanent—it is the now attained vocabulary wherein both the new ways of saying can be undertaken, and the inverse hermeneutic of reinterpreting the world can be performed.

This is to say, that once the structure or the field of possible contexts is open, the phenomenological attitude provides the way to explore possibilities which is its field. In the edifying sense, this means the exploration is one which seeks *to find what intuitions can be constituted.* And it is here that variational method emerges as the central driving engine of an edifying phenomenology.

Before following that implication, I would like to take note of one fundamental difference between Rorty's "hermeneutic" and a phenomenological one. Phenomenology has never been simply a linguistic philosophy. Although there are strong variants, with Husserl and Merleau-Ponty as "perceptualists," with Heidegger and Gadamer more "linguistic." In all cases what counts as language is always experiential, and even better, perceptual. In phenomenology it would better be termed a language-perception pairing. Even Dasein is concretely bodily-spatial and *Being and Time* rather than merely talking about how one is to perform a phenomenololgy, undertakes it in relation to human spatiotemporality. But it must be understood that perception here means the perception of phenomenology ("lived body," "lifeworld," "time consciousness," etc.) and not that of Cartesian or Modern, neo-Cartesian physicalism.

In fact, the language-perception link in phenomenology is also tied to both context relativity and to variational praxis. For example, if intuitions are constituted, not simply given, then the task for variational explorations will be to find out in what situations, contexts, cultures, times, "x" intuition can or will occur. This is an actual hermeneutic investigative practice. Husserl preferred fantasy or imaginative variations, and through his midcareer he simply accepted the (false) empiricist assumption that imaginative variations could simply substitute for any other kind, particularly the perceptual kind (imagination duplicates perception). This practice, modelled upon mathematical procedures, but also a favored shortcut for abstract and writing-room-bound philosophers, was thought to be sufficient to yield the invariants of the field of possibilities.

The post-Husserlians challenged this limitation upon variational investigation and developed other practices. Merleau-Ponty (with a different cognate disciplinary background, psychology) noted that perceptual variations could not be substituted for by imaginative ones and developed this inquiry most thoroughly in *The Phenomenology of Perception*. And in a more historical vein, Heidegger took the same tack with respect to his variant *epochs* of Being. Here were historical—and in the case of his "Conversation with a Japanese"—cultural variants. In each case the phenomenology involved, particularly as a practice, uncovered or hermeneutically exposed how the "intuitions" are constituted by the context. For Merleau-Ponty the context is motile bodily position with its interaction with the environment; for Heidegger it is the constellation of historical beliefs which sediment and account for some (then or now) current state of affairs.

Interestingly, this insight and practice derived directly from Husserlian phenomenology, and in spite of explicit rejections of "phenomenology," continues brilliantly as *praxis* in both Derrida and Foucault! For example, in an earlier piece, I have shown how Derrida is doing something of a standard phenomenology of reading in his play upon margins and the like:

> Take a text: If one views a text (perceptually) it usually appears first as a writing that is centered on the page, surrounded by margins; but the focal center is clearly the bulk of what is written. Then, if one reads the text, what usually emerges as focal is what the text is about, however complex that may be, as indeed any text usually is. What does Derrida do with a text? Posed in the way I have indicated, he immediately decenters what seems to be focal and immediate. His focus is radically shifted to titles, signatures, margins, borders, divisions, etc. In short, he draws our attention to features that are there, but are usually taken at most as background, secondary, or unimportant features.
>
> In a sense this is a highly 'phenomenological' technique. For example, in an analysis of perception, phenomenologists like to point out that while what stands out (figures) are usually most obvious because they are the referenda of our usual perceptions, all figures take their position upon a background that is equally present and that constitutes the field of perceivability. In short, this move 'decenters' focal perception so as to attend to taken-for-granted but important fringe features. Similarly, to point out that all perceptions include not only manifest surfaces, but latent 'backsides,' is to 'decenter' at least the usual interpretations *of* perception. I am suggesting that his device—perhaps taken to Nietzschean

excess—is a familiar ploy of Derrida. Indeed, one can see, once the operation is known, how to follow along with such deconstructions. (Is there a Derrida text that addresses itself to the empty background of the page? If not, there ought to be.)[14]

Foucault, too, continues the *praxis* of some distinctly phenomenological habits even while linking phenomenology with Husserl and opposing it. His unmentioned teacher, Merleau-Ponty,[15] remains his subterranean mentor. Foucault does histories of perception, as in the *Birth of the Clinic*. That is to say, he traces the radically different ways things are seen in correlation to the different practices of an epoch. (Foucault has a miniversion of Heidegger's epochs of Being, but Foucault's are smaller, more discrete, more rapid in change.) This praxis which continues the development of contexts of language-perception is perhaps most dramatic in *The Order of Things*. Not only is his outline a subtle response to Merleau-Ponty (who claimed there could be language about language, but not painting about painting. *The Order of Things* begins with Velázquez's "Las Meninas," a painting about painting.) The intricate pairing of experience in language-perception is precisely the forte of Foucault who may have adopted unconsciously the phenomenological vocabulary, but who *does* what I would term a kind of subterranean edifying phenomenology.

If, in Husserl's case, phenomenological edification is implicit, and if in the post-Husserlians the scaffolding and transcendentalism places existential and hermeneutic phenomenology on at least a nonfoundationalist trajectory, and if what unites this development is a certain *praxis* which may be either implicit or explicit, then, once having taken Rorty's shift seriously, the question can become more explicitly that of the possibility of an edifying phenomenology.

There may be a quibble here: why call it phenomenology? Heidegger ceased to use the term. Derrida and Foucault, by linking it to the foundationalist, transcendental enterprise, reject it. But if the trajectory I have outlined obtains and the *praxis* underlies what I would term an extension of variational method is the case, then there is at least more continuity than is usually allowed. Perhaps what is suggested is a *new* version of phenomenology, an edifying phenomenology which has at its core precisely that hermeneutic and inverse hermeneutic performance which freely explores what Rorty calls the exotic (histories, cultures, disciplines, etc.).

A (New) Phenomenology which Edifies

What I have been suggesting is that phenomenology in the late twentieth-century—whether it is called that or not—has had a more and more non-foundationalist trajectory. Both the explicit transcendentalism of Husserl and the vestigial foundationalism of an early Heidegger have given way to the now dominant strains of hermeneutics and post-structuralist enterprises of the present. Perhaps out of some unsuspected conservativism, but more likely out of a philosophical preference of actional (as opposed to epistemological) analyses, I have chosen to retain the ancestral name.

The same applies to the occasions represented here. A collection by its very nature is not a systematic or accumulative development. It, rather, presents themes, examples, applications. which are united only by the unconscious vocabulary of a style—but which better would be seen as vectors along a trajectory. Husserl taught us *how* to do phenomenology. But once learned, the scaffolding which allowed one to get at the edifice is seen to be secondary. Different values about what is central emerge.

Phenomenological *praxis*, I would contend, revolves around an active variational inquiry. Variational inquiry may be imaginative, perceptual, historical-cultural, or interdisciplinary. It thus looks a bit like what Rorty calls hermeneutic or edifying philosophy. But also because variational inquiry is linked to a sense of experience with its language-perception pairing, there is a certain perspective upon things. It is a perspective which links a sense of *position* (from where are things seen? the vestiges of noesis) *referred* to a *context* or field (what and how do the things, old or new, appear?). But it is not tied to any preferred foundation. To be sure, if variations are perceptual, there is the privilege of the lived or motile body, but if they are intersubjective, imaginative or whatever else, that focus is displaced.

Between the extended Introduction and now this brief response to Rorty, the collected chapters are attempts to follow the trajectory of a nonfoundationalist phenomenology. I take this to be following *consequences* of phenomenology. The thematic occurrences of plays upon gestalts, the development of cultural-historical variants upon the perceptions of technology, the cases of context relative phenomena are examples along this line. Yet, while such a phenomenology may be nonfoundational and hermeneutic in at least Rorty's sense, it also may give the appearance of having a vestige of the previous past.

Phenomenology, even if nonfoundationalist, remains *structural*. But its structuralism is of an odd sort. Within its chosen field of investigations—contexts of possibility which constitute possible experiences of the language-perception type—its still essentially investigative thrust is one which discovers (vestiges of truth seeking) a multiplicity of structures. I return once more to the notion of multistability to make the point.

Structures discovered are not all of one type. In the often used examples of visual multistability in the preceding chapters, I would contend that the structure of possibility is linear and arbitrary (contrary to Merleau-Ponty). But such a possibility structure in no way exhausts the possibilities of others. Were one to move from the abstract, two-dimensional drawing examples, to concrete, three dimensional objects in

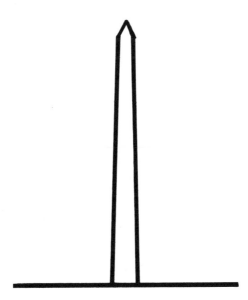

the normal earthbound context, one might discover a structure of *graded* possibilities.

Vary the Washington Monument: Its current stability is upright.

This actual stability, without changing its architecture, would be even more stable, hence a graded possibility, were it to lie on its side on the level ground:

And under some temporary conditions it *might* even be (barely) stable upside down and perfectly balanced:

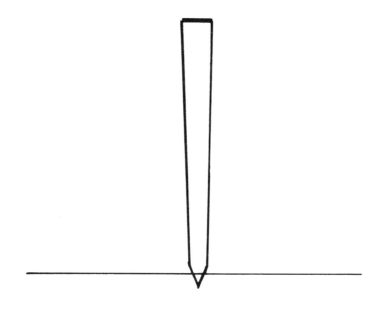

But this last possibility is clearly gradedly weaker than either of the first two, while other possible positions are so weak as to be impossible (without changing the structure of the Monument itself):

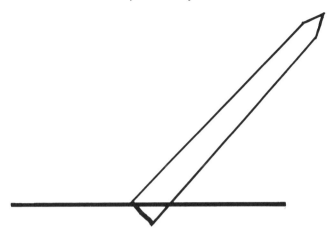

Still other types of structural stability could be hierarchical, serial, independent/dependent, etc. If this is vestigial "foundationalism" it is both oddly so, since the investigation and horizontalization of the field of structure is neither selective (all are context relative) nor reductive (there is no "best" or "only" structure). But it does come short of the one aspect of Rorty's conversations which place him much closer to the newer French versions of Continental philosophy than the older phenomenological ones.

By removing both truth seeking and referentiality entirely from edifying philosophy, Rorty joins the ranks of the post-structuralists and deconstructionists who have, while genuinely creating a new type of historical and cultural "science," also simply sidestepped the possibilities of what I prefer to call a *noematic* science. (The natural sciences, interestingly enough, come closer to this sense of phenomenological praxis—of the investigation of possible structures—than the previous human sciences.) This is in no way to deny what Kuhn and the new philosophy of science has discovered; that the practice of the sciences falls under essentially hermeneutic interpretations, that science itself includes an inevitably hermeneutic dimension, and so forth. But the need for the "outward" look, the noematic reference, is implicitly the retention of the language-*perception* pairing found within phenomenology.

Phenomenology insofar as it is essentially hermeneutic is edifying in Rorty's sense. That is, it is non-foundational in its newer and post-Husserlian forms. But it is also edifying in a stronger sense for it is not without "edifice," *structure*. Finally, while phenomenology does have its vocabulary, it also retains its perceptions.

Notes

Introduction

1. What Rorty terms the Analytic-Continental split is in fact deeper, particularly in its political ramifications. In recent years what has become known as the Pluralist Movement has grown to a significant challenge to the largely analytic dominance of the Eastern Division of the American Philosophical Association. This movement had its origin in the controversies surrounding the State Education Department reviews of doctoral programs in New York State. While I cannot quote from the documents I am referring to it is well known that the rating committees made the claim that phenomenologists in particular were not qualified to teach in such areas as philosophy as metaphysics, epistemology or ethics because their only "area" was phenomenology. This gross misunderstanding may have been the result of cultivated ignorance or deliberate political intention, but often remains institutionalized in APA classifications. (Phenomenology, like analytic philosophy, is a way of doing philosophy—but the subject matter in either case may be ethics, epistemology or metaphysics, etc.)

2. Richard Rorty, *Consequences of Pragmatism* (Minneapolis: University of Minnesota Press, 1982), pp. 223-24.

3. Adolf Grünbaum, "Freud's Theory: The Perspective of a Philosopher of Science," *Proceedings and Addresses of the American Philosophical Association*, September, 1983, Vol. 57, pp. 5-31.

4. During my graduate years in the Boston area, with the exception of John Wild in his last years at Harvard, there was

virtually no phenomenology taught. Sam Todes and Hubert Dreyfus were, however, instructors at M.I.T. where I initially met them.

5. Both phenomenology and positivism were originally dominated by refugee scholars. In an excellent study, Lewis Coser has traced this development in philosophy. Herbert Feigle, Hans Reichenbach, Rudolph Carnap, Carl Hempel, Kurt Goedel, are but some of the names in this list. Similarly, refugees were among the first to bring phenomenology to this country. See Lewis Coser, *Refugee scholars in America: Their Impact and Their Experiences* (New Haven: Yale University Press, 1984). Interestingly, the same phenomenon applies to France—early phenomenology there was taught primarily by refugees from Germany and eastern Europe. See Bernard Waldenfels, *Phänomenologie in Frankreich* (Frankfurt: Suhrkamp Verlag, 1983).

6. Herbert Spiegelberg, *The Phenomenological Movement*, Vol. II (The Hague: Martinus Nijhoff, 1960), pp. 626-7.

7. A much more thorough account of Farber's influence may be found in "Marvin Farber's Contribution to the Phenomenological Movement: An International Perspective," by Helmut R. Wagner in *Philosophy and Science in Phenomenological Perspective* edited by Kah Kyung Cho (The Hague: Martinus Nijhoff, 1984), pp. 205-236. It may be noted that Cho, educated and primarily published in Germany, today is Farber's virtually sole phenomenological successor at S.U.N.Y. Buffalo.

8. Gurwitsch did not actually move to the New School until 1959—thus even this center barely gelled before the sixties.

9. Lewis Coser, *Refugee Scholars in America: Their Impact and Their Experiences* (New Haven: Yale University Press, 1984), p. 297.

10. Hugh Silverman has, as much as anyone, called notice to the Americans in the recent generations of phenomenology. In a 1980 article, "Phenomenology", *Social Research*, Winter 1980, Vol. 47, No. 4, he traces a history much broader than the one I am undertaking here. But of particular interest is his own characterization of those phenomenologists who began developments here. I quote in anticipation of my own list to follow:

> Still others conducted their research entirely within an American context. In following the program set by Husserl and his existential successors, these philosophers examined specific issues or questions. Instead of opening up whole domains of research, they apportioned their concerns by addressing precise topics, such as language (James M. Edie),

embodiment and its implications for medicine (Richard Zaner), the human senses and their equipment (Don Ihde), the libidinal expressions of the body (Alphonso Lingis), imagination and memory (Edward S. Casey), the passions (Robert C. Solomon), the history of philosophy (John Sallis), autobiographical consciousness and objectivity (William Earle), freedom, being and the human sciences (Calvin O. Schrag), the foundations of the social sciences (Maurice Natanson), and so on, pp. 713-4.

Silverman is also the author of a second brief study, "The Continental Face of Philosophy in America", *Philosophy Today*, Winter 1983, pp. 275-80.

11. Janice Moulton, quoted by Rorty, *Consequences of Pragmatism*, p. 230.

12. Although humanists tend to be unaware of it, much interesting information may be found in both the Humanities and Social Science citation indices. One can find who and what is being discussed (beware self-citers for inflationary tendencies). Careful inspection will show not only what writers are currently being cited, but from what quarters. For example, certain AEE philosophers are cited almost entirely within a small set of philosophy journals, in contrast to most well known ACE philosophers who are sometimes even dominantly cited interdisciplinarily.

13. Giants are easily recognized in the *Indices* since their citations occupy several columns. Silverman makes one of the criteria of philosophical style what he calls "reference texts". Of ACE writers he notes, "The reference texts tend to be quite determinate and distinctively different from those of analytic philosophies". "The Continental Face of Philosophy in America", p. 278. One might add that too often these reference texts are in effect, *reverence texts*!

14. Since the movement to pluralize the Eastern Division of the APA opened both the nomination committee and the presidency to elections, there have been three non-analytic results in the last few years. John Smith and Quentin Lauer and Joseph Kockelmans have achieved this elective status.

15. James Edie in an address to the Society for Phenomenology and Existential Philosophy, St. Louis, 1983, scheduled to appear in *Research in Phenomenology*, Volume XIV.

16. Because I am concentrating upon American "Continentals," I have not mentioned some of the frequent and even regular visitors from the Continent, some of whom serve as the primary or only such

representative in certain universities. Dieter Hendrich at Harvard, Dagfin Follsdall at Stanford are examples.

Chapter 2

1. Maurice Merleau-Ponty, *Essential Writings*, edited by Alden Fisher (New York: Harcourt, Brace and World, Inc., 1969), p. 48.

2. *Ibid.*, p. 49

3. Maurice Merleau-Ponty, *The Visible and the Invisible*, translated by Alphonso Lingis (Evanston: Northwestern University Press, 1968), p. 212.

4. Although the group of Continentally oriented philosophers in the Stony Brook Department is currently the largest such group in the US and they span the entire range of interests mentioned here, the particular focus upon a multidimensional and polymorphic perception has been most emphasized by my colleague, Patrick Heelan, and myself. See his *Space Perception and the Philosophy of Science* (Los Angeles: University of California Press, 1983) and my *Experimental Phenomenology* (G.P. Putnam's Sons, 1977).

5. A.T. Aveni, "Tropical Archeoastronomy," *Science*, 10 July 1981, Vol. 213, No. 4505, pp. 161–171.

Chapter 3

1. At the actual event where this paper was first presented, the session at Temple University on phenomenology as a type of interpretation, I had with me a styrofoam cube, a construction as suggested below, and a drawing of a Necker cube. Here, in written form, such artifacts could be pictured (at greater production costs) and even could be sent along with each publication to recapture some of the full perceptual experience. Yet, that does not often happen and because this is unlikely, we can also see that there is normally a vast difference between the presentation of an oral and a written paper. The perceptual context is changed and with it, I would claim, the significance and hermeneutic problem of the situation.

2. A much fuller examination of the structure of possibilities implied in multistable drawings may be found in my *Experimental Phenomenology* (Putnam's, 1977).

3. As indicated, I had such a construction at the original presentation. The two-dimensional effect could, however, be

obtained in a number of different ways without such an elaborate artifact. For example, were I to describe the Necker cube as a drawing of an insect hanging onto the edges of a hexagonally shaped hole with the central configuration the body and the six lines the legs, the two-dimensionality of the drawing would appear.

4. Again perceptual clues are useful in distinguishing the differences as suggested above. An even greater difference, however, may be noted temporarily between speech and writing.

Chapter 4

1. Lucretius, *On The Nature of the Universe*, trans. by R.E. Latham (Middlesex: Penguin Books, 1975), p. 28.

2. *Ibid.*, p. 29.

3. *Ibid.*, p. 96.

4. Francis Bacon, *The Dignity and Advancement of Learning* (London: George Bell and Sons, 1901), p. 383.

5. *Ibid.*, p. 383.

6. Christopher Marlowe, *Doctor Faustus* (New York: Appleton, Century, Crofts, 1950), p. 5.

7. Lynn White, Jr., "Cultural Climates and Technological Advance in the Middle Ages", *Viator*, Vol. 2, 1971, p. 174.

8. Martin Heidegger, "The Question Concerning Technology", *Basic Writings*, trans. by David Krell (New York: Harper and Row, 1972), p. 302.

9. *Ibid.*, p. 304.

Chapter 5

1. Don Ihde, *Technics and Praxis* (Dordrecht: Reidel Publishers, 1979) and Friedrich Rapp, *Analytical Philosophy of Technology* (Dordrecht, 1981)

2. See *Technics and Praxis*, chapter 10.

3. Martin Heidegger, "The Question Concerning Technology", *Basic Writings* edited by David Krell (New York: Harper and Row, Publishers, 1977), pp. 283–318.

4. Lewis Mumford, *Technology and Human Development* (New York: Harcourt, Brace and Co., 1971).

5. Thomas Gladwyn, *East is a Big Bird* (Cambridge: Harvard University Press, 1970).

6. A. T. Aveni, "Tropical Archeoastronomy," *Science*, 10 July 1981, Vol. 213, No. 4504, pp. 161–171

7. *Ibid.*, pp. 163–4.

8. Ihde, *Technics and Praxis*, pp. 6–11.

Chapter 6

1. Ortega y Gasset, *The Modern Theme*, trans. James Clengh (New York: Harper and Brothers, 1961), p. 1.

2. *Ibid.*, p. 1.

3. Ortega y Gassett, *The Idea of Principle in Leibniz and the Evolution of Deductive Theory*, trans. Mildred Adams (New York: W.W. Norton & Co., 1971), p. 248n.

4. *Ibid.*, p. 322n.

5. *Ibid.*, p. 283.

6. *Ibid.*, p. 287n.

7. Ortega y Gasset, *Phenomenology and Art*, trans. Philip W. Silver (New York: W.W. Norton & Co., 1975), pp. 30–31.

8. *Ibid.*, p. 24.

9. *Leibniz*, op. cite., p. 304n.

10. *Ibid.*, p. 281n.

11. Ortega y Gasset, *What is Philosophy?*, trans. Mildred Adams (New York: W.W. Norton & Co., 1960), p. 218.

12. Ortega y Gasset, *Meditations on Quixote*, trans. Evelyn Rugg and Diego Marin (New York: W.W. Norton & Co., 1963), p. 45.

13. *Ibid.*, p. 45.

14. *Ibid.*, p. 34.

15. *Ibid.*, p. 53.

16. Perspectivism, Ortega's derivation from a perceptual model, plays a definitive role in his aesthetics and philosophy of history, and may be deemed a phenomenological strategy of his work.

17. *What is Philosophy?*, op. cite., p. 96.

18. *Leibniz*, op. cite., p. 140n.

19. *What is Philosophy?*, op. cite., p. 198.

20. *Ibid.*, p. 199.

21. *Quixote*, op. cite., pp. 41, 45.

22. *Phenomenology and Art*, op. cite, p. 110n. Here we find evidence that Ortega, particularly in his own later self-interpretation, is *not* the best interpreter. He claimed not to have been familiar with Dilthey whose thinking is so close to Ortega, until 1933. Yet this quotation citing *Erlebnisa* from Dilthey is from 1916!

23. *Leibniz*, op. cite., p. 280n.

24. *Ibid.*, pp. 280–281.

25. *Phenomenology and Art*, op. cite., p. 62.

26. *Leibniz*, op. cite., p. 280n.

27. *Phenomenology and Art*, op. cite., p. 63.

28. *Leibniz*, op. cite., p. 280n.

29. *Phenomenology and Art*, op. cite., p. 66.

30. *Ibid.*, p. 23.

31. *Ibid.*, p. 23.

32. *What is Philosophy?*, op. cite., p. 199.

33. *The Modern Theme*, op. cite., chapter one.

34. *Phenomenology and Art*, op. cite., pp. 26–27.

35. *Ibid.*, p. 27.

36. *Ibid.*, p. 27.

37. Ortega y Gasset, *The Origin of Philosophy*, trans. Toby Talbot (New York: W.W. Norton & Co., 1967), pp. 14–15.

38. *Ibid.*, p. 21.

39. *Ibid.*, p. 151–152.

40. *Phenomenology and Art*, op. cite., p. 151.
41. *Ibid.*, p. 152.

42. *Ibid.*, p. 153.

43. *Ibid.*, p. 159.

44. *Ibid.*, p. 160.

45. *What is Philosophy?*, op. cite, pp. 245–246.

46. *Ibid.*, p. 246.

47. *Ibid.*, p. 185.

48. *Ibid.*, p. 185.

49. *Ibid.*, p. 186.

50. *Ibid.*, p. 68.

Chapter 7

1. Paul Ricoeur, *The Symbolism of Evil*, trans. Emerson Buchanon (New York: Harper and Row, Publishers, 1967), p. 4

2. *Ibid.*, p. 6

3. *Ibid.*, p. 7

4. *Ibid.*, p. 7

5. *Ibid.*, p. 7

6. *Ibid.*, p. 7

7. *Ibid.*, p. 10

8. *Ibid.*, p. 9

9. *Ibid.*, p. 11

10. *Ibid.*, p. 16

11. *Ibid.*, p. 8

12. *Ibid.*, p. 7–8

13. *Ibid.*, p. 15

14. Paul Ricoeur, *The Rule of Metaphor*, trans. Robert Czerny (Toronto: University of Toronto Press, 1977), p. 317

15. *Ibid.*, p. 317

16. *Ibid.*, p. 321

17. *Ibid.*, p. 322

18. *Ibid.*, p. 322

Chapter 8

1. Robert Nozick's *Philosophical Explanations* was the year's contender. But if my small sample is indicative, whereas Rorty was read, Nozick's tome rarely was finished by readers.

2. I continue the convention of the Introduction here with ACE meaning the American Continental Establishment and AE the Analytic Establishment.

3. Richard Rorty, *Philosophy and the Mirror of Nature* (Princeton: Princeton University Press, 1979), p. xiii.

4. Others are also aware of the need to recharacterize the practice of analytic philosophers, as in Moulton's use of a legal practice.

5. I have long contended that Husserl must be read-through. His heuristic discourses on method are attempts, after he has seen something difficult to see, to tell others how to do it. By adopting extant terminologies and then reversing or radically changing their meanings, his work is almost metaphorical. Heidegger, I would contend, must be read *literally*.

6. To term these gestalts and imply Husserl used them is a bit anachronistic since the Gestaltists were aware of and in some cases were students of Husserl.

7. Rorty, *op. cite.*, p. xiii.

8. Privately circulated, this list apparently came out of one of the Dreyfus summer programs.

9. A current dissertation by Gary Aylesworth traces both the Wittgensteinian and Heideggerian directions carefully (Stony Brook, 1984).

10. Rorty, *op. cite.*, p. 394.

11. *Ibid.*, p. 360.

12. *Ibid.*, p. 360

13. See my "Phenomenology and the Later Heidegger," which shows the way in which phenomenology functions in his later works (in *Existential Technics*, SUNY, 1983).

14. Don Ihde, "Phenomenology and Deconstructive Strategy," *Semiotica*, 41 (1982), pp. 8-9. (Also reprinted in *Existential Technics*.)

15. Chapter two of this collection goes into more detail on Merleau-Ponty and Foucault.

Index

208